50

SUFISM

ALSO BY NASROLLAH S. FATEMI:

Life of the Persian Poet Hafiz
Diplomatic History of Persia
Oil Diplomacy
Dollar Crisis
Problems of Balance of Payment and Trade (Editor)
Sufi Studies: East and West (Contributor)
Multinational Corporations

SUFISM

Message of Brotherhood, Harmony, and Hope

Nasrollah S. Fatemi
Faramarz S. Fatemi
Fariborz S. Fatemi

SOUTH BRUNSWICK AND NEW YORK:
A. S. BARNES AND COMPANY
LONDON: THOMAS YOSELOFF LTD

A. S. Barnes and Co., Inc.
Cranbury, New Jersey 08512

Thomas Yoseloff Ltd
108 New Bond Street
London W1Y OQX, England

Library of Congress Cataloging in Publication Data

Fatemi, Nasrollah Saifpour, 1911–
Sufism: message of brotherhood, harmony, and hope.

Includes bibliographical references and index.
1. Sufism.   2. Sufi poetry, Persian—History and
criticism.   I. Fatemi, Faramarz S., joint author.
II. Fatemi, Fariborz S., joint author.   III. Title.
BP188.9.F37   297'.4   75-29692
ISBN 0-498-01869-5

PRINTED IN THE UNITED STATES OF AMERICA

To Fairleigh S. Dickinson, Jr., whose deeds and acts represent an example of what the Sufis call a real human being.

Contents

Acknowledgments

My grateful thanks are due to my good friend Idries Shah, the leading exponent of Sufi ideas in the world today, for his gracious encouragement; to Professors Heinz Mackensen, Ben Nelson, Theodore M. Chesler, and Edna Charles for reading the book and making useful suggestions; to Audrey March for reading through and editing the manuscript; and to Sandra Asdoorian and Marion Johnson for their work in typing and checking documents.

Our sincere thanks are due to the following authors and publishers whose works and words are quoted in this volume.

Messrs. George Allen and Unwin for passages from all the works and translations of A. J. Arberry, Reynold A. Nicholson's *Rumi, Poet and Mystic*; Cyprian Rice's *The Persian Sufis* and *Rumi Discourse*; Edward Rehatsek's *Gulistan Sadi*; Cambridge University Press for passages from the first edition of E. G. Browne's *Literary History of Persia*, Volume III; Reynold Nicholson's *Divan Shamsi Tabriz* and a *Literary History of the Arabs*, and *Eastern Poetry and Prose;* The Dial Press, Thomas Mann, *The Permanent Goethe*; Columbia University Press, Majid Fakhry's *A History of Islamic Philosophy*; Everyman's Library, A. J. Arberry, *Persian Poems*; Tudor Publishing Company, *The Works of Ralph*

9

Waldo Emerson; Philosophical Library, Dagobert D. Runes, ed., *Treasury of Philosophy*; The MacMillan Company, Philip Hitti's *History of the Arabs*, first edition, A. J. Arberry, *Classical Persian Literature*; Clarendon Press, G. M. Wickens's *Legacy of Persia*; Barrie and Jenkins Ltd., Inayat Khan's *Sufi Message*, Volume VI; Mentor Books, Stephen Spender, *Great Writings of Goethe*; University of Oklahoma Press, A. J. Arberry, *Shiraz Persian City of Saints*; Teheran Press, R. Z. Shafaq's *Tarikh i Adabiyat Iran*, Hedayat's *Majmaul Fasaha*, *Badey uz Zaman, Mulana Rumi*; Rutledge and Kegan Ltd., Reynold Nicholson's *The Mysticism of Islam*; Lucknow Publishing House John A. Subhan, E. J. Brill, William McKane, trans., *Al-Ghazali, Book of Fear and Hope*; Luzac and Company, T. J. DeBoer, *The History of Philosophy*, and Al-Ghazali's book of the Ihya; Margaret Smith's *The Sufi Path of Love* and *Al-Ghazali, The Mystic*; Octagon Books, Inc. Edmund Gardener's *Dante and the Mystics*; Oriental Translation Fund for James Atkinson's translation of *Laili and Majnun* (Nizami); UNESCO and Teheran University for the use of their archives on the collection of Persian Series; Harvard University Press, Karl Vietor, *Goethe the Poet*; J. T. Foulis and Co., Louisia Stuart Costello, *The Rose Garden of Persia*; The University of Chicago Press, Van Grunbaum's *Medeivale Islam*; Fisher Unwin of London, for E. G. Browne's *A Literary History of Persia*, Vol. II; S. C. Griggs & Co., Chicago, for Elizabeth Reed's *Persian Literature*; J. M. Dent & Sons, London for E. Pocock, *Persian Poems*; Duckworth and Co. Ltd., London for Richard Le Gallienne, *Odes From the Divan of Hafiz*; Ministry of Education, Iran, for Dr. Ghani's *Divani Hafiz*; The International Library of Famous Literature, *Johan Goethe*; Bombay Press for James Atkin's translation of *Laili and Majnun*; Iranshahr Press, for *Chahar* Maqaleh, and Madras S.P.C.K. Depot, for Rev. E. Sell's *Essays on Islam*; Oxford University Press, *The Legacy of Persia*, A. J. Arberry (editor, 1953) Trubner and Co., for passages from E. H. Winfield's translation of *Shabistari's Gulshan i Raz*; Routledge and Kegan Paul for passages from Whinfield's translation of Khayyam's Quatrains; Mr. John M. Watkins for passages from Khayyam's Quatrains and *Odes of Hafiz*; Frank Cass and Co., for *Oriental Mysticism*, first edition; George Bell and Sons Ltd., for the R. A. Nicholson's *The Mystics of Islam*, first edition; E. P. Dutton & Co. for the publication of A. J. Arberry's *Rubaiyat of Omar Khayyam and other Persian Poems*.

There are other older writers and translators to whom we are indebted and we would like to express our most sincere gratitude and thanks.

Since there is no uniform transliteration of Persian and Arabic words, we have followed the Persian pronunciations, and in quotations we have used the style of the original authors.

Introduction

The elements common to Judaism, Buddhism, Christianity, and Islam can best be appreciated in Sufism, "which bear equal testimony to that ever-deepening experience of the soul when worshippers turn wholeheartedly to God."

Sufism has been defined as both "the apprehension of divine realities" and as "a universal message of love, brotherhood and unity of man." It is not a religion; it does not create another church or a new sect, but attempts in the words of Rumi, "to eliminate conflicts, feuds, fights and to unite people in love and harmony."

Sufism is an idealistic pantheism. It has two sides, the one philosophic, the other mystic. The Sufis see their God directly. He is the absolute Truth, absolute good, and absolute beauty. His Divine nature could be discovered through transcendental meditation, self-negation, love of mankind, gnosis, and service.

The subject of Sufism is so multidimensioned that many large volumes would be required to do it any justice. In this first of three volumes, we have tried to sketch a broad outline of certain principles and doctrines and translations of some of the works of five of the best-known Persian poets. "Difficult and long are the paths which we tread, dark and hidden are our pathless destination," but even if we may not be able to accompany the travelers to their journey's end yet we hope to give them a glimpse of the Sufi's spiritual experience, intellectual environment and their contribution to the Persian culture and literature.

The Sufis' aim was to introduce an ecumenical spirit and spiritualize and purify the Islamic establishment from within, to give it deeper mystical interpretation and infuse into all religions a spirit of love and liberty. These lofty ideas were disseminated mainly through Persian and Arabic poetry. Sufism produced great names and famous poet-preachers who roamed a vast area of the world from Spain to Indonesia. Names like Al-Ghazali, Rumi, Al Junayd, Ibni Arabi, Dhul Nun, Hafiz, Sadi, Mansur al Hallaj, Nizami, Omar Khayyam, and Khalil Jaobran and Iqbal are known not only in the Islamic world but even beyond it.

Every nation has a literature peculiarly her own, even if it has been influenced by foreign sources. As the universal empire of Iran was founded upon the ruins of more ancient monarchies and as she gathered into the halls of her palaces the spoils of the conquered nations, so also was her literature enriched by the philosophy, science, poetry, and mythology of her predecessors. The mind of Persia from the very beginning was a universal one. Cyrus the Great, the founder of the empire, based his rule on tolerance and respect for other cultures and religions. The blooming of the Persian mystical mind and of universal ideas may be placed around the fifth century B.C. However, the golden age of the Persian literature and poetry starts with the ninth century A.D. The Persians of this period seem to have been born with a song on their lips, for their distinguished Sufi poets are many, and their philosophical, mystical, and spiritual contributions are enormous.

This volume gives only a glimpse into the life, the times,

and the work of five of the most distinguished Sufi poets:
Rumi, the prince and the light of Sufism; Hafiz, the idol of
Persian-speaking people; Sadi, the wisdom of Sufism and
the spokesman for reason, moderation and universal
brotherhood; Nizami, the symbol of love and tenderness
("Not all the treasured lore of ancient days, can boast the
sweetness of Nizami's lays"); and Omar Khayyam, that
conscience of Sufism whose songs and philosophy have
enchanted millions of people over five continents.

The real dream of the Sufis was expressed by Rumi: "not
to foster, but rather to heal the schism between minds as
they looked upon the disputes of the numerous Muslim,
Jewish and Christian sects." This hope of reconciliation
was included in the Sufi dogmas:

(1) There is no God but God, the All Merciful and the All
compassionate.

(2) The ways to reach Truth(God) are as numerous as the
number of people on the surface of the earth. There is one
way of reaching truth, the annihilation of false pride and
ego, and following the path of selflessness and service to
our fellow men.

(3) There is one law, the law of reciprocity. A peaceful and
harmonious life with our fellow men can be led only when
the sense of justice has been awakened in us by a selfless
conscience. The sense of justice is awakened in a perfectly
sober mind that is free from the arrogance of power,
wealth, command, birth, and rank. The world is happy and
harmonious when justice is the dominant power.

(4) There is one brotherhood, the human brotherhood,
which unites all people of the world indiscriminately in the
fatherhood of God.

(5) There is one morality, the love that springs from self-
denial and blooms in deeds of service to mankind. Love is a
healing physician, capable of healing all wounds and recon-

ciling all feuds. Its compassion turns fighting foes into friends and makes saints out of sinners.

(6) There is one Truth, the true knowledge of our being, within and without. Know thyself, and thou shalt know God. It is the knowledge of self that blooms into the knowledge of God.

This modest contribution is appearing at a time when people throughout the world are praying for an end to the religious feuds and ideological conflicts that have brought war, devastation, and deprivation to so many nations. The authors hope that this study may contribute to a better understanding among people of different cultures and backgrounds.

The purpose of this volume is not to cover the Sufi world or present stories of sects, cults, and orders, their rites and rituals, but is intended to introduce the American reader to a new interpretation of Sufi ideas and thoughts and some aspects of their universal and humanistic culture.

This introduction could not be concluded without expressing our sincere thanks to Farivar S. Fatemi, Assistant Professor of History and Political Science at Bergen Community College, for his valuable assistance in the research of this volume.

Nasrollah S. Fatemi

SUFISM

1
The Rise of Sufism

All sects but multiply the I and Thou;
This I and Thou belong to partial being;
When I and Thou and several beings vanish,
Then Mosque and Church shall bind thee never more,
Our individual life is but a phantom:
Make clear thine eye, and see Reality!

Go soul! with Moses to the wilderness
And hear with him that grand 'I am the Lord;'
While, like a mountain that shuts out the sun,
Thine Eye lifts up its head; thou shalt not see me,
The lightning strikes the mountain into ruins
And o'er the levelled dust the glory leaps!

Shabastari

The modern world stands at the threshold of perpetual
crisis. As a result of two global conflicts and many years of
cold war, troubled men and women all over the world are
experiencing a twofold need. They feel the need for a new
vision of the world, a clearer insight into the fundamentals
of moral and spiritual values. At the same time, they seek

19

peace of mind through deeper understanding of other cultures and civilizations.

The great spiritual movements in history have taken place during eras of stress and strife. Confucius, Buddha, the Prophets of Israel, Zoroaster, Socrates, Plato, Jesus, Muhammad, and other great thinkers and leaders appeared during periods of trial and discord when people suffered disillusionment, frustration, and mistrust and when spiritual and moral anarchy prevailed. In the history of the Muslim world, the Sufi writers and thinkers played a significant role during the period of greatest stress. Their movement was a rebellion against a society very similar to that of our times—suffering from arrogance, conflict, dishonesty and moral decadence.

In the one hundred years between the death of the Prophet Muhammad and the Battle of Tours in A.D. 732, the Muslim army had conquered the Iberian Peninsula, North Africa, Syria, Iraq, Persia, and Central Asia. During this period of expansion the seat of power was transferred from Madineh in Arabia to Kufeh in Iraq, then to Damascus in Syria. In 762 Baghdad was selected as the new capital, and the empire rose to the zenith of its material prosperity and cultural splendor. In less than fifty years Baghdad grew from a village to a world capital of prodigious wealth and international significance. Its splendor kept pace with the prosperity of the upper class who dominated this vast empire. It was the center of wealth, learning, power, commerce, and virtue, but it also became the hub of vice, crime, and corruption.

The royal palace occupied one-third of the round city. Particularly impressive was the audience chamber decorated with the most lavish rugs, curtains and cushions that the Orient could produce. The Caliph's wife, who would tolerate no tableware not made of gold or silver and studded with gems, set the fashion for the "sophisticated," and she is remembered as the first in her time to ornament her shoes with precious stones.[1] During one holy pilgrimage she was reported to have spent three million dinars, which included the lavish expense of supplying Mecca with water during a season of drought. Yet this is not an isolated example of the extravagance that prevailed during the Golden Age of Islam.

Although there were millions of poor in the empire, the marriage ceremony of the Caliph Al Mamoun was celebrated in 825 with such fabulous festivity that it is listed in Arabic literature as the unforgettable extravagance of this golden era. On the night of the wedding a thousand pearls of enormous size were showered upon the newlyweds, who sat on a golden mat studded with precious jewels. A 200-rotl*** candle of ambergris turned night into day. Balls of musk, each containing a ticket bestowing an estate or a slave or some other precious gift, were presented to the guests.[2]

In 917 the Caliph Muhtadi received with great pomp the envoys of Constantine VII whose mission evidently involved the exchange and ransom of prisoners. The Caliph's procession included 160,000 cavalry and military footmen, seven hundred black and white eunuchs, and seven hundred chamberlains. In the parade marched a hundred lions, and in the Caliph's palace hung thirty-eight thousand curtains, of which twelve thousand were gilded, and there lay twenty-two thousand rugs. The envoys were so struck with awe and admiration that they mistook first the chamberlain's office and then the vizier's for the royal audience chamber. In time the ambassadors were seated in a hall, with the Tigris River on the one side and the royal gardens on the other. The hall was curtained and carpeted throughout.

The envoys were finally delivered into the presence of the

Caliph, whom they found seated on his throne with his sons on either side of him. Then the ambassadors were given a tour of the palace grounds to deepen their impression of the wonders—especially the royal zoo containing various kinds of animals, including elephants and lions.

> Later the ambassadors were shown the "Palace of the Tree" wherein they found a tree standing in the midst of a great circular tank filled with clear water. It had eighteen branches, every branch having numerous twigs on which sat all sorts of gold and silver birds, both large and small. Most of the branches were of silver, but some were of gold and they spread into the air carrying leaves of diverse colors. The leaves moved as the wind blew while the birds piped and sang. On the other side of this palace, to the right of the tank, were the figures of fifteen horsemen mounted upon their mares, and both men and steeds were clothed in brocade. In their hands the horsemen carried long-poled javelins, and those on the right were all pointed in one direction (it being as though each were attacking his adversary); for, on the left-hand side, was a like row of horsemen.[3]

Like magnets the Abbasside rulers of the ninth and tenth centuries attracted to Baghdad poets, wits, musicians, singers, dancers, trainers of hunting dogs and fighting cocks, and others who could amuse, interest, or entertain. Siyat and Ibn Jami led the roster of musicians and singers. Caliph Amin (r. 809–13) one evening bestowed on a professional singer the sum of 300,000 dinars for singing one song. Amin also had a number of special barges shaped like animals built for his parties on the Tigris. One of these vessels looked like a dolphin, another like a lion, a third like an eagle. The cost of the barges to the poor people and the empire was 3,000,000 dirhams.[4] When the Caliph arranged for a picturesque all-night ballet, scores of beautiful girls danced in rhythmic unison to the soft harmony of the music and were joined in their singing and dancing by all those who attended.[5]

The libertine poet Abu Nuwas, the boon companion of the Caliph and his courtiers on many a nocturnal adventure, depicted in most vivid language the court life of the period. The pages of *Al Afghani* likewise abound with illustrative love stories whose nucleus of truth is not hard to discern.

A jester at the court of Caliph Harun, Abu Nuwas was a poet of extraordinary genius. In his wine songs, with an art almost Greek in its ease and directness—he paints a society dominated by luxury, debauchery, corruption, and cruelty. He ridicules the convention of Bedouin love-poetry and the rude monotony of life in the desert. He treats tradition, religion, and moral laws with contempt. His writing reflects the mood, the way of life and manners at the Court of Baghdad:

> Four things banish grief and care,
> Four sweet things incline
> Body and soul and eye
> To enjoy, if they be there:
> Water, wine,
> Gardens bright and faces fair.

> Youth and I, we ran
> No recorded sin
> of the gifts of Time
> Than when music wakes.
> O the girl whose song
> Oft at sunrise
> Make the most of youth,
> Let the wine flow round
> Pour into thy cup
> That will melt to ruth
> Sought and chosen out

> Dower'd with twin delights
> Seest not thou that I
> Kissed the mouth of fair
> 'Tis because I know,
> Far apart shall be.[6]

2

Aside from the Caliphs, the members of the royal family, the viziers, the aristocrats, and the officials, functionaries, and other satellites of the court also indulged in extravagant living. But for the common man life was hard. While the rulers of Baghdad were steeped in luxury, pomp and splendor, the dying empire was caught in a net of Sybaritism. Abandoned was the pietist tendency of early Islam. The piety, poverty and temperance of the first four Caliphs were replaced by lust, luxury, power, privilege and despotism in an empire which had lost connection with Islam.

Forgotten was the injunction of the Prophet that "through piety are souls brought to perfection, and persons may compete for excellence in it; and let him who desires honor seek it in piety."[7]

We have the words of two famous writers of the eighth and ninth centuries concerning the decline of Islam as a religion and the rise of the Muslim Empire. Al Kharraz, the famous mystic of the ninth century, describes the virtues of Islam under the immediate successors of the Prophet in the following words:

> When Abu Bakr (r. A.D. 632–36) succeeded to the leadership, and the world in its entirety came to him in abasement, he did not lift up his head on that account, nor make any pretensions; he wore a single garment, which he used to pin together so that he was known as "the man of the two pins." Umar Al Khattab (r. 634–44)

who also ruled the world in its entirety, lived on bread and olive oil; his clothes were patched in a dozen places, some of the patches being of leather; and yet there were opened unto him all the treasures of Chosroes and the Caesars. As for Uthman (644–54), he was like one of his slaves in dress and appearance; of him it is related that he was seen coming out of his gardens with a bundle of firewood on his shoulders and, when questioned on the matter, he said, "I wanted to see whether my soul will refuse." When Ali (656–61) succeeded to the rule he bought a waistband for four dirhams and a shirt for five dirhams; finding the sleeves of his garments too long, he went to a cobbler and, taking his knife, cut off the sleeve level with the tips of his fingers; yet this same man divided the world right and left.[8]

However, by A.D. 790, Ahmad of Antioch was lamenting the empire's decline into the evils of luxury. He gives a vivid picture of how, in less than a quarter of a century after Muhammad's death, all the virtues of Islam were replaced by the corruption of a heartless empire:

Now I will tell a tale of long ago,
How first the faith began, and how it grew
To full perfection; yet, and I will tell
How next it withered till it hath become
E'en as a faded garment. After this
I have for thee a very gem of knowledge
Which thou canst gain, if thou will heed my words,
A knowledge copious, to scour the heart
Of stain and rust, and make it clean and bright.
True is my knowledge, clear and eloquent,
Precious as pearls and rubies of great price;
By grace Divine I indicate the truth,
Being taught by God Himself, for that I live
Within an age become exceeding strange,
Cruel and terrible, wherein we need
Most urgently a statement of our faith
And intellectual arguments thereto:

Islam hath been most nobly eulogized
As mourners praise the dear departed dead.[9]

At the time when Ahmad made this statement the Islamic
world had developed into a class-structured society, a new
society which had very little in common with the community
which Muhammad had preached.

The Abbaside rulers in 803 recognized four classes of
people:

1. The ruler, whom merit had placed in foremost rank;
2. The Chancellor (Grand Vizier) and his civilian and
   military aides, distinguished by wisdom and discrimi-
   nation;
3. The aristocracy and religious leaders (*ulama*);
4. The small middle-class composed of businessmen,
   musicians, teachers, and craftsmen who were attached
   to the court.

Members of the royal family, officials, and functionaries,
following the example of the caliphs, lived in luxury. Caliph
Haroun's mother had an income of 160 million dirhams.
(DIRHAM was the principal silver coin, worth one tenth of
a DINAR. A Dinar was a coin containing 45 grams of gold.)
When one of the tax collectors died he left 50 million
dirhams in cash.

"An idea of the fortunes amassed by the Rothschilds and
Rockefellers of the age may be gained from the case of the
Baghdad jeweller Ibn-al Jassas, who remained wealthy after
the Caliph had confiscated 16 million dinars of his property."[10]

Caliph Haroun's half sister Ulayyah, in order to cover a
blemish on her forehead, used a fillet set with most precious
jewels. Soon the fillet was adopted by the rich ladies of
fashion in Baghdad as the most cherished ornament.

This privileged group was composed of a very small

minority of upper-class aristocracy, intellectuals, theologians, artists, and merchants; but the rest of the people—99 percent of the subjects of the Caliph—were living in poverty and misery with few rights and little voice in the affairs of the state.

Social, political, and economic changes transformed the primitive tribal system and the simple, virtuous, puritan, and spiritual world of the Prophet Muhammed. Many voices were raised against the corruption of religion, tyranny, and the exploitation of man. The following two popular songs of the time are an expression of the sentiments of a people who resented their society with its misery and immorality:

> Sons of concubines have become
> So numerous amongst us,
> Lead me, O God, to a land
> Where I shall see no bastard.

No, certainly, I shall not pray to God, as long as I shall be poor.
Let us leave prayers to the high and mighty,
To the chief of the armies, whose cellars bulge with treasures.
But why should I pray? Am I mighty? Have I a palace, horses, rich clothes and golden belts?
To pray when I do not possess a single inch of earth would be pure hypocrisy.

3

It was at the height of this moral decadence and social injustice that the Sufis raised their voices. Their movement, originating as a protest against the formalism of orthodoxy in Islam, gradually developed into a rebellion against the decadence, corruption and tyranny of a sick, material society. Sufism was the antithesis of arrogance, intolerance, demagogism, hypocrisy, and inhumanity. The Sufis' purpose was to create a renaissance of man's spirit through which he might live a simple, innocent, happy and harmonious life. They hoped to open men's eyes, that they might see that egoism, greed, pride, and strife are folly; that the universe is spiritual, and that men are the sons of God. The Sufis agreed with St. Paul that "the fruit of the Spirit is love, joy, peace, long-suffering, gentleness, goodness, faith, meekness, temperance."[11]

Few terms in the dictionary of Islam are as impressive as the term "Sufi" or "Sufism." Its very mention often provokes debate about its meaning, its evaluation, and its purpose. To the orthodox and traditional Muslims, it stands for qualities deeply distrusted and despised. To some, it connotes humanitarianism, tolerance, harmony, defiance of the church and its rituals, love of mankind, and the attempt to achieve spiritual fellowship. To a few, the Sufis are dreamers, rebels, and meddlers who interfere with the serious rituals of the church and the business of the state. To others, they are the conscience of society and the antennae of the community, who exhibit in their activities a pronounced concern for humanity and a deep interest in the values that lie at the core of society, and who accuse the civil and religious authorities of lacking social conscience. The Sufis felt the need to resist the corrupt, tyrannical, and arrogant society, to ridicule the cruel rich and the merciless might, to exalt the low, and to help the helpless. They turned their eyes to the huge masses of simple, poor, ignorant people. For during this so-called golden age of the Baghdad civilization, the rich became richer and the poor became poorer, and "the vessel of the state was driven between the Scylla and Charybdis of anarchy and despotism." A minority of rich people ruled a huge empire of millions of poor peasants and slaves. These people accepted poverty, hunger, ill-treatment, disease, and suffering with resignation. They accepted the whip of the agents of the caliphs and the empty words of the church as a preordained fate. They accepted their Hell as did Milton's Satan:

> So farewell hope, and, with the hope farewell fear,
> Farewell remorse! All good to me is lost;
> Evil, be thou my good. . . .

The Sufis considered this situation reprehensible and risked imprisonment and even death by protesting against the materialism, indifference, extravagance, and inhumanity of society. They tried to attack the hypocritical pretension of the church; they tried to introduce people to the realms of "inner thoughts and values." The questions they repeatedly asked were: "Is God merely the object of formal worship or of love?" "Isn't the purpose of religion to unite, to comfort, to improve, and to bring all races and peoples of the world together in love and brotherhood, or is it to divide, to tyrannize, to shed the blood of the innocent in futile wars, to mesmerize, to commit all kinds of crime in the name of Allah and to exploit our fellowmen?" The God of Islam, they reminded society, is supposed to be compassionate, all-loving, all-merciful. He tells us, "Do not despair of my mercy. Despairing of love and mercy is a greater fault than your sin."[12] Everything in this world—folly and wisdom, power and impotence, wealth and poverty, happiness and sadness, glory and humiliation—is but empty and transitory without love and involvement. Everything in this life is mortal, except God and good deeds. The guiding principles of the Sufis shifted emphasis from the external rituals of religion to the mind and heart, to inward worship, to the service and brotherhood of man. Unquestionably, these divine injunctions of love, service and brotherhood were nowhere amongst the Muslim sects so well heeded and preached as among the Sufis.

Sufism throughout the centuries has been a source of inspiration to poets, a fountain of ideas to many thinkers, and a treasury of wisdom to the sages and savants of the East. Its realm is the whole universe. It goes beyond religion, ideology, color, creed, or race. "It follows the religion of love."

One of the most persistent doctrines of Sufism was inwardness. They despised outward piety and shallow religious rituals. "Direct thyself to the inward and thou shalt see thy God," they said. "Strive to cleanse thy heart from greed and hatred and transfer it to compassion, service and love of your fellowmen. Service and ideas prepare you for eternal felicity, as the world with its ephemeral values can never do. As for fame, it is fleeting. As for riches, they are disappearing. As for beauty and youth, they are vanishing. The body may die, but ideas and service will survive." Therefore, a Sufi's goal was to make himself capable of eternal felicity and salvation. This could be achieved by dedicating one's life to the service of mankind and protection of one's life against the seductions of vanity, greed, arrogance, and glory.

The Sufis, in the words of Hakim Sanai,[13] were looking for "the ocean of love, and they did not bother with the rivers and canals of conflict and prejudice. Their mission was to bring unity, brotherhood, hope and happiness to the family of man. Their purpose was to help a generation which was suffering from the ills of mistrust, materialism, prejudice, and conflict."

1. Masudi, vol. VIII, pp. 298–99, translated by Philip Hitti, *History of the Arabs*, sixth edition, London. Macmillan & Co., Ltd., 1956.
2. Tabasi, vol. III, pp. 1081–84, translated by Philip Hitti, Ibid.
***A rotl was a weight used in Iran and the surrounding countries and is equal to one pound.

3. *Al-Hatib al-Baghdadi*, translated by G.A. LeStrange, quoted by Gustave E. Von Grunebaum, *Medieval Islam*, pp. 28–29, University of Chicago Press. 1945
4. Tabasi, *op. cit.*, pp. 951–53.
5. Philip Hitti, *History of the Arabs*, pp. 302–05.
6. Reynold A. Nicholson, translation of *Eastern Poetry and Prose*, London, Cambridge University Press, 1922, pp. 29–30.
7. Baidowi, quoted by Gustave E. Von Grunebaum, *Medieval Islam*, 1945
8. Kharraz, *Kitab al-Sidq*, translated by A. J. Arberry, *Sufism*, George Allen and Unwin Ltd., London, 1950, p. 32.
9. *Ibid.*, p. 31.
10. Baidowi, *op. cit.*
11. Galatians 5: 22–23.
12. *Qoran* 39:54
13. Hakim Sanai of Ghazni (d. 1150) was a Sufi poet and mentor. He introduced the doctrine of "Unity" practiced by men of enlightenment, or gnostics, who enjoy union with God.

2

The Evolution of Sufism

Sufism is freedom and generosity and absence of self-constraint. Sufism is control of the faculties and observance of the breaths. Sufism is wholly self-discipline. It is Sufism to put away what thou hast in thy head, to give what thou hast in thy hand, and not to recoil from whatsoever befalls thee.

The origin of the word "Sufi" has been the object of much dispute. Some Sufis maintain that it is derived from the Arabic word *Safa* meaning "purity." Others contend that it is an historical allusion to *Ashabus-sufa* or to the people of the bench, referring to the fact that the early Sufis spent most of their time debating the orthodox clergy on benches at the porch of the Mosque. However, the majority of scholars today agree that the name is derived from *suf* (wool). The Sufis wore coarse woolen robes and lived as hermits in isolated places away from the people and believed in salvation through poverty (*Fagr*), meditation (*Fikr*), fortitude (*Sabr*), renunciation (*Zuhd*), good works, and service to the community. Recognizing that God's presence was felt everywhere in creation, they became increasingly mystical, pantheistic, and ascetic.

For Rabia, one of the founders of Sufism who died at

Jerusalem in A.D. 757, love and its unquenchable flames were the torch which kindled the world of Sufism. It was she who laid the foundation of its mystical ideas. She was succeeded by Abu Hasham (d. A.D. 770), who established the first convent (Khaneqah) for the Sufis at Ramaleh in Palestine. Soon the movement spread to Persia. "Hand in hand with the Persian revival under the Abbaside Caliphs the Sufis developed a new current of ideas. Speculation takes a bolder flight, and essays to reconcile the creature with his creator, to bridge the chasm between the finite and infinite."[1]

Then followed the doctrine of ecstasies, mystical stages, unification and pantheism. Though the Sufis always confessed outward connection with orthodox Islam, nonetheless they would effectually undermine its foundation. They attacked the religious institutions by claiming that religion exists only to keep mankind in order and to make all men merit the grace and love of God by their service and virtues. Every religious institution which does not tend toward these goals is not divine but profane and dangerous. Scorning the barren desert of legalistic tradition, meaningless rituals, and the hypocrisy of the clergy, admitting no guidance but the pole star of illumination, they pressed the Islamic establishment to the very brink of madness. The Muslim leaders considered Sufism a grave scandal, demoralizing the national character, undermining law and order and subverting traditional society. Yet the Sufis produced a literature and a doctrine of universalism and love which is considered the noblest heritage and the greatest contribution of Persia to world civilization.

2

Hassan al-Basri, an early spokesman for the movement, condemned worldly possessions: "Two bad companions, the dinar and dirham [gold and silver]. They profit you only when they have you." (In the Sufi world it was not so much poverty that was desirable as freedom from avarice.) The Prophet Muhammad had stated that he was proud of his poverty, for the rich man was tied to this world with stronger cords than the poor. The renunciation of material wealth and personal power was considered the greatest virtue.

While the Sufis condemned cupidity and greed, they also abhorred begging and laziness. "God expects his children to work for their provisions. Every prophet has had work as a shepherd." Muhtasibi, describing the early Sufis, wrote: "The believer who is seeking for godliness renounces all that is destructive to him in this world and the next, and leanness is manifest in him, and mortification and solitude and separation from the companionship of the pious, and the appearance of grief and absence of joy, and he chooses all that, hating to indulge in pleasure which may incur the wrath of the Lord and make him worthy of his chastisement."[2]

Despite heretic tendencies, the early Sufis remained generally firm in their adherence to orthodoxy. Even Al-Junayd, who had sown the seeds of a unitary mysticism conditioned by Hindu concepts of the self, did not draw all the possible consequences that later and bolder spirits were to draw.[3] Later on Sufism added to qoranic teachings many elements of theosophical and pantheistic doctrines; in Sufism there is the fundamental concept of God as not only All Mighty and All Good, but as the sole source of Being and Beauty and indeed the one Beauty and the one Being, in whom is submerged whatever becomes apparent, and by whose light whatever is apparent is made manifest.

In the words of Evelyn Underhill (1875–1941), "Sufism is the passionate longing of the soul for God, the unseen reality, loved, sought and adored in himself alone. It is a metaphysical thirst." A Sufi is not a person who practices unusual forms of prayer, but one whose life is freed from avarice, selfishness, and hatred. He feels and responds to the overwhelming attraction of his Creator and the service of his fellow creature.

Sufism is that form of life in which, under the negation of the world and "I," the complete union of the soul with God is longed for and striven after as the *summum bonum*. Leave yourself outside, it advises, and then go in.[4]

3

On the basis of Neo-Platonic ideas, the Sufis attributed reality to God. Man participates in reality only to the extent that he has attained identification with God. Not only is man created in the image of God and His representative on earth but, according to the Qoran, even before anything else was made, man made an eternal covenant (*Misaq*) to worship his Creator who is immediately close to him as the only God: "So your Lord told the angels: 'I am creating a human being out of clay. When I have shaped him and breathed my spirit into him, fall down on your knees before him.'"[5]

The Sufis believed that there was an element of reasonableness in man's nature which worked towards human solutions to problems. So it was that the prophets did not come to make life more complicated, but to make life easier for all of us. The only reason for the existence of religion is to guide, to help, to harmonize, and to unite mankind. Its goal should be the establishment of a world brotherhood. "The ways unto God are as numerous as the number of people living in this world." (Tariqt-ullah Kal-adadi Nufusi Bani Adam.)

When Abu Said, one of the leaders of the Sufis, was asked to define the Sufi doctrine, he replied: "It is to lay aside what you have in your head such as pride, prejudice, desire, hostility, greed, arrogance, and hatred; to give away what you have in your hand; and to flinch not from whatever befalls you. The veil between God and thee is neither earth nor heaven, nor the throne nor the footstools; thy selfhood and hate are thy veil, and when thou removest these and replace them by love, thou hast attained unto God."[6]

The Sufis habitually rejected the doctrine of "the fear of God, the wrath of the day of Judgment, the fury of Hell and the promise of Heaven." Faith based on coercion is slavery, and God has created man with mind, free will, and love. Therefore, the mainspring of Sufism is love—not fear and obedience to a church.

"Love is the mood of the Sufi, gnosis his aim, ecstasy his supreme experience." Love, according to Ali Gushairi, is a noble state of mind in which goodness reveals itself. God loves man and man loves Him. Love leads to gnosis or the meeting of the Friend and is the first step in establishing fellowship with Him.

The Sufis, like St. John of the Cross, cried:

O living flame of love
That, burning, dost assail
My inmost soul with tenderness untold,
Since thou dost freely move,
Deign to consume the veil
Which sunders this sweet converse that we hold.
How tender is the love
Thou wak'nest in my breast
When thou, alone and secretly, are there.
Whispering of things above,
Most glorious and most blest,
How delicate the love thou mak'st me bear.

Junaid states that the love of God is the center of our soul, the resting place of our desires and the sphere of our love. Jalaluddin Rumi, apostle of the Sufi Doctrine, eulogizes the Sufi idea of love in the following verse:

Hail to thee, O love, our sweet melancholy
Thou physician of all our ills,
Thou purge of our pride and conceit,
Thou are our Plato and our Galen.
Our earthly body, through love, is raised to the skies,
Mountains take to dancing and to nimbleness.
Love became the soul of Sinai, lover.
Sinai was intoxicated and Moses fell swooning.
Its secret is hidden 'twixt topmost treble and lowest bass,
Were I to reveal it I'd shatter the world.
But, were I close to my confidant's lips,
I would, like the reed-pipe, say all my say.
He that is far from men that speak his tongue
Is speechless, though he have a hundred voices.
When the rose is gone and rose-garden fallen to ruin,
Whence wilt thou seek the rose's scent? From rose water?
The All is the beloved and the lover a veil,
The living is the beloved and the lover a thing dead.
When love no more has this attraction,
It remains like a bird without power of flight.[7]

Sufism is knowledge of oneself which leads one to *Marafat* (gnosis) or knowledge of God. Man's whole life is dominated by two realities: "Thou" and "I": the lover and the beloved, God and man. Nasir Khosrow, the famous Persian poet (A.D. 1004–88), referring to the knowledge of one's self states:

Know thyself, for knowing truly thine own heart
Thou knowest that good and ill in thee are part.
Discern the worth of thine own being, and then
Walk with pride amidst the common run of men.
Know thyself, and the whole world thus discover,

Then from all ill, they shall thyself deliver,
Thou knowest not thyself for thou art lowly,
Thou shouldst behold God if thou thyself couldst see.

Forever associated with the supreme values of love and gnosis is the doctrine of *Fana* (self-effacement). There are three stages, according to Rumi, for the cleansing of the soul: abandonment of evil qualities, concentration on good deeds, and contemplation of the divine. Here one detects the influence of Plotinus (A.D. 205–270): "The soul thus cleansed is all idea and reason, wholly free of body, intellect; entirely of that divine order from which the wellspring of beauty rises and all the race of Beauty . . ."

Finally, the Sufis believed in union (*Wasl*) with God. This is the stage of ultimate satisfaction because the Sufi has submitted himself to the will of God. At this stage he decides to serve God as his divine beloved and to devote his life to the service of mankind. It is in this last stage that the Sufi claims to experience meditation, nearness to God, love, hope, longing, service, intimacy, tranquility, and contemplation. The Sufis believed that "states" eventually descend from God into man's heart and that the seeker experiences only those states which God chooses to bestow upon him. After completing all stages of the path, the Sufi is transformed from "seeker" to "knower" and reaches a new plane of consciousness which is called "gnosis." This is a stage marked by the deepest understanding of the divine knowledge of God.[8] At this stage the Sufis, like Mansur Hallaj,[9] exclaim: "I am he whom I love, he whom I love is I; we are two souls, endwelling in one body. If thou seest me thou seest Him and if thou seest Him thou seest me."

1. R. A. Nicholson, *Divani, Shamsi Tabriz*, Cambridge University Press, 1898, p. xxviii.

2. Von Grunebaum, Gustave E., *Medieval Islam*, The University of Chicago Press, 1945, p. 132.

3. Fakhry, Majid, *A History of Islamic Philosophy*, New York, Columbia University Press, 1970, p. 271.

4. *Rumi*, translated by Cyprian Rice in *The Persian Sufis*, George Allen and Unwin Ltd; London, 1964, p. 61.

5. *Qoran*, 38:71–72.

6. R. A. Nicholson, *Literary History of the Arabs*, 2nd ed., Cambridge University Press, 1930, p. 234.

7. *Rumi*, translated by R. A. Nicholson.

8. Subhan, John A., *Sufism—Its Saints and Shrines*, Lucknow Publishing House 1932, pp. 68–73.

9. Mansur Hallaj was a Sufi saint who was crucified for his defiance of orthodox Islam in Baghdad in A.D. 922.

3

The Sufi Contribution to the World of Ideas

"People are subject to changing 'states,' but the Sufis have no 'state,' because their vestiges are effaced and their essence annihilated by the essence of another, and their traces are lost in another's traces."
Abu Ali of Sind.

A Sufi is one who conceives of life as an experience in eternity—one who holds that the soul, even in this life, can unite itself with the Divine. He calls himself *Ahl al-Haqw*, the seeker of the truth. The early Sufis were ascetics and quietists rather than mystics. However, in the beginning of the ninth century they developed an ecumenical doctrine based on the ideas of Zoroastrianism, Buddhism, Judaism, Christianity, Neoplatonism, and Islam. Sufism regards all religions as more or less "perfect shadowings-forth of the great central truth which it seeks fully to comprehend, and consequently it recognized all of them as good in proportion to the measure of truth which they contain."

The great practical aim of Sufism is to escape from selfishness, and until this goal is attained, no advance towards truth can be made. Sufis regard God as identical with pure Being. Sufism, therefore, is considered to be an idealistic pantheism: Everything is God.

It was the Egyptian philosopher Dhul Nun (d. 861) who introduced the idea of gnosis (*Marifat*) into Sufi doctrine. Born of a Nubian slave, Dhul Nun was a Renaissance man. He was well-versed in philosophy, law, literature, alchemy, ancient Egyptian history and hieroglyphics. His writings show a knowledge of Hermetic wisdom. Considered to be the first Sufi *qutb* (the pillar of the universe) and the first exponent of theosophy, Dhul Nun was to Sufism what St. Paul was to Christianity. He introduced the idea that true knowledge of God is attained by means of ecstasy (*Wajd*).

Furthermore, Dhul Nun states that gnosis (*Marafat*) is God's providential communication of the spiritual light to our inmost hearts. "He who belongs to God and to whom God belongs is not connected with anything in the universe."[1]

The following prayer of Dhul Nun is a good indication of his pantheistic tendencies:

O God, I never hearken to the voices of the beasts or the
rustle of the trees, the splashing of waters
or the song of birds,
the whistling of the wind or the rumble of thunder,
but I sense in them a testimony to thy unity (*Wahdanyya*),
and a proof of the Incomparableness; that thou art
the all-prevailing, the all-knowing, the all-wise,
the all-just, the all-true, and in Thee is neither
thoughtlessness nor ignorance nor folly nor injustice
nor lying.

O God, I acknowledge Thee in the proof of Thy hand-
iwork and the evidence of Thy acts; grant me, O God, to
seek Thy satisfaction with my satisfaction, and the Delight

of a Father in His child, remembering Thee in my love
for Thee, with serene tranquility and firm resolve![2]

In his poetry Dhul Nun uses the language of the devoted
lover:

> I die, and yet not dies in me,
> The ardour of my love for Thee,
> Nor hath Thy love, my only goal,
> Assuaged the fever of my soul.
>
> To Thee alone my spirit cries,
> In Thee my whole ambition lies,
> And still Thy wealth is far above
> The poverty of my small love.
>
> I turn to Thee in my request,
> And seek in Thee my final rest;
> To Thee my loud lament is brought,
> Thou dwellest in my secret thought.
>
> To Thee alone is manifest
> The heavy labor of my breast,
> Else never kin or neighbours know
> The brimming measure of my woe.
>
> Guidest Thou not upon the road
> The rider wearied by his load,
> Delivering from the steeps of death
> The traveller as he wandereth?
>
> O then to me Thy favor give
> That, so attended, I may live,
> And overwhelm with ease from Thee
> The rigor of my poverty.[3]

Asked about the qualities of the gnostics, Dhul Nun
answered: "The gnostics see without knowledge, without
information, without description, without unveiling, and

without veil. They see God in everything. They move as
God causes them to move; their words are the words of
God; their sight is the sight of God. God through his
prophets tells us: 'When I love a servant, I, the Lord am his
ears, so that he hears by Me; his eyes, so that he sees by Me;
his tongue, so that he speaks by Me, and his hand so that he
takes by Me." Dhul Nun once asked a woman what was the
end of love. "Thou fool!" she replied, "Love has no end,
because the Beloved is eternal."

Shabastari, another Sufi teacher, argues that if it was possible for Moses to talk to God through a burning bush,
other men may surely do the same.

Come into the valley of peace, for at once
The bush will say to Thee, 'verily I am God';
The saying "I am God' was lawful for the bush,
Why should it be unlawful for a good man to say so?[4]

Bayazid of Bistam (d. 875) is regarded by many as one of
the founders of the pantheistic school. He was the grandson
of a noted Zoroastrian, and his Sufi teacher was Abu Ali of
Sind. Bayazid in all his teachings identified himself with
pantheism. He stated in public: "Beneath this cloak of mine
there is nothing but God." He embarrassed his Sufi brethren and scandalized the orthodox by exclaiming: "Glory to
me! How great is my majesty! Verily I am God! There is no
God beside me, so worship me."

On another occasion Bayazid declared that a single atom
of the sweetness of love and knowledge of God in a man's
heart is better than a thousand palaces in paradise. Knowledge without love and service is useless.[5]

The doctrine of *Fana Fellah* (Self-absorption in God)
from Bayazid's time onward assumed a central position in
the structure of Sufi theory. "All this talk, turmoil, rites,
ritual, conventions, customs, noise and desire," according to

Sufis, "is outside the unity with God; remove the veil of dualism then you will find joy, silence, beauty, calm, and rest. When you unite with your Beloved then there is neither command nor prohibition."[6]

This was a transition from the Sufi doctrine that all else but God is nothing to the theory that when self as well as the material world have been cast aside the Sufi will unite with God. "I, we, Thou, He are all one thing, for in unity is no duality." There is egoism in every act of man; egoism is dualism. All that exists is learned in two ways, according to Bayazid: by abandoning self-interest and following God's commands of loving one's fellowmen.

Bayazid never followed formal religious rites and rituals. When someone asked him why he did not attend prayer services in the mosque, he answered, "I have no leisure to pray; I am roaming the spiritual world, and whenever I see anyone fallen and in need of my service, I do my best to help him." On his way to Mecca Bayazid met a man who asked where he was going. When Bayazid told him his destination, the man asked him how much money he would spend. "Two hundred dirhams," was Bayazid's estimate. The stranger suggested that since he had no income to support his wife and children, Bayazid should pay him the two hundred dirhams and instead of walking seven times round the blackstone of the Kaaba, he should walk round him, thus completing his pilgrimage. Bayazid accepted the offer, paid the money to the stranger and returned home.

In the work of another Sufi teacher, Ibrahim Ebn Adham, Prince of Balkh (d. 777), the son of the Viceroy of Khorassan, we find the influence of Buddhism. He had spent his life in luxury and laziness. Like Buddha, one day when he was chasing a fox, he heard a voice behind him saying, "It was not for this thou wast created; it was not this thou wast charged to do." When he continued his chase, he heard another voice, clearer than before. "O Ibrahim! It was not for this thou wast created. It was not this thou wast charged to do!" He considered this a warning, returned home, abandoned his horse and joined his father's shepherds in the mountains. Later he left Khorassan, roaming from place to place seeking peace of mind. Finally in Syria he came in contact with some Christian monks from whom he learned how to make peace with himself and his Creator.

When a friend asked Adham for a definition of worship he replied: "The beginning of worship is meditation and silence, then follows recollection (*Dhikr*) and service to your fellow man." When one of his disciples told him that he was studying only rhetoric, Adham commented, "You are in greater need of studying silence and working to help your fellow men." His favorite prayer was: "O God, Thou knowest that paradise weighs not with me so much as the wing of the gnat. If Thou befriendest me by Thy recollection, and sustainest me with Thy love, and makest it easy for me to obey Thee, then give Thou paradise to whomsoever Thou wilt."

The similarity of Sufi views to the philosophy of universalism proved attractive to the Persian Shiahs amongst whom there was a strong gnostic element. Bored with the dry formalism of rigid law and a stiffened ritual, these Persians discovered in Sufism a welcome idea. "In Sufism," states A. J. Arberry, "we have what is generally regarded, and not without much justice, as the supreme manifestation of the Persian mind in the religious sphere."[7] The hard and fast system of Shariah (Islamic Law), the rigid dogmas of the clergy and the finality of their doctrine and law were alien to the flexible minds of the Persians. In the Sufi concept of "the soul's exile from its maker and its inborn longing to return and lose itself in Him" they found a doctrine which saved them from the inadequacies and barrenness of orthodoxy. The latter represented Allah as having created the world once for all and then having removed himself to heaven, leaving his creatures to work out their own salvation or condemnation, according to the light given them by the prophets. The Sufis, in sharp contrast, represented Him as the Sublime Being, immanent and ever working in His creatures, the sum of all existence, the fullness of life, whereby all things move and exist, not only predestining but originating all actions dwelling in and terminating with each individual soul. The Sufi believed that he would see his God face to face in everything, and in seeing Him, would become one with Him. His God was his friend.

G. M. Wickens writes:

> At that depth genuine Persian Sufism is not to be distinguished from our own Western mysticism, and Al-Ghazali, by God's grace, loves his Lord and is loved by Him no less than St. Francis, Rabiah, no less than St. Teresa of Avila. . . . But the Sufis, like the great Greek thinkers, whose heirs in many senses they were, lacked the twin anchors of the Fall and the Incarnation. . . . The ostensible mystery of the Trinity was in fact much more nearly apprehended by them than as by other non-Christians.[8]

The Sufis were content to borrow from Neoplatonism, Judaism, Christianity, and Manichaeanism, but to live and work within the framework of Islam according to the commands and prohibitions of the Qoran. Their aim was to present to the world a universal idea infused with spiritualism, love, and liberty. Furthermore, they strove to free man from institutional shackles, hypocrisy, and rigid rules, and open a new world subject to the honesty and purity of spirit and heart. This new faith "was disseminated mostly by poetry, it breathed in an atmosphere of music and song. In it the place of great dogmatic treatise is taken by mystical romances. Its one dogma, an interpretation of the Muslim witness: 'There is no God but God,' is that the human heart must turn always, unreservedly, to the one, divine, beloved."[9]

3

Another of the Sufis' important contributions to Islam was the elaboration of the idea of pantheism. They combined mystical love and compassion with a daring challenge to rigid and hypocritical religious rules and rituals. Their God was real, they could see Him in every noble, decent, compassionate man and woman. Everything beautiful, lovely, and adorable represented the Sufi God.

Baba Kuhi of Shiraz (d. A.D. 1050), a contemporary of Abu Said, another great Sufi teacher, explained the Sufi theory of pantheism and unity with God in the following verses:

In the market, in the cloister—only God I saw.
In the valley and on the mountain—only God I saw.
Him I have seen beside me oft in tribulation;
In favour and in fortune—only God I saw.
In prayer and fasting, in praise and contemplation,
In the religion of the prophet—only God I saw.
Neither soul nor body, accident nor substance,
Qualities nor causes—only God I saw.
I opened mine eyes and by the light of His face around me
In all that eye discovered—only God I saw.
Myself with mine own eyes I saw most clearly,
But when I looked with God's eyes—only God I saw.
I passed away into nothingness, I vanished,
And lo, I was the all-living—only God I saw.

Hussein Ibn Mansur Hallaj (d. 932) declared that when

man is so absorbed in his divine Beloved that he abandons
self and becomes conscious only of his God, then he is one
with God:

> Swift for Thy sake, I sped over land and sea
> And clove a way through world and steep, heartfree,
> And turned aside from all I met, until
> I found the shrine where I am one with Thee.[10]

Hallaj, walking through the streets of Baghdad, told his
listeners to stop wasting their time and money by attending
services in the mosques or making pilgrimages to Mecca in
search of God. He admonished the citizens for dishonesty
in their daily lives. He accused the authorities and
businessmen of robbing orphans and old women and asked
them to spend their money on the poor and the sick and to
look for God in their hearts. "Cleanse your heart! Dedicate
yourselves to the service of your people," he said.

According to Hallaj, man is essentially divine because he
was created by God in His own image. The doctrine of
incarnation (*Hulul*), a cardinal tenet of both Hallaj and
Bayazid Bastami, held that the Sufi must lose himself entirely in divine unity. This teaching—a fusion of old pre-Islamic
Persian beliefs and Neoplatonic theory—is "an extremely
interesting illustration of the combination of Oriental and
Hellenistic elements in Sufism. In this case whatever they
may borrow from Persia and India receives its interpreta-
tive hypotheses from Neoplatonism."[11]

When Hallaj was brought before the Inquisitor and
commanded to repent for his beliefs, his answer was: "I am
He whom I love, and He whom I love is I. We are two spirits
dwelling in one body. If thou seest me, thou seest Him and
if thou seest Him, thou seest us both."[12]

In 922 Hallaj was crucified for claiming identity with
God, and thereafter Sufism became more and more openly

identified with pantheism and gnosticism. The legend of his death, which attributes nobility and magnanimity to him, is similar to the Christian story of the Crucifixion:

> When he was brought to be crucified and saw the cross and the nails, he turned to the people and uttered a prayer ending with the words: 'And these Thy servants who are gathered to slay me, in zeal for Thy religion and in desire to win Thy favor, forgive them, O Lord, and have mercy upon them; for verily if Thou hadst revealed to them that which Thou hadst revealed to me, they would not have done what they have done; and if Thou hadst hidden from me that which Thou hadst hidden from them I should not have suffered this tribulation.'[13]

According to the Sufis, good and evil are inevitably and intimately linked: One must have knowledge of evil in order to perceive the existence of goodness. The Sufis looked therefore to a higher good, the Absolute, uncontaminated by association with evil. To be one with ultimate good is to divest oneself of all evil, of all malicious earthly influence and above all, of one's selfish tendencies. It is in self that utter evil resides. It is interesting how near to Manichean ideas the Sufis are, remembering that both Manicheanism and Sufism were nurtured in Persia.[14]

4

Sufis divide God's creation into the perceived world and the conceived world. The former is the material, visible world, familiar to all men; the latter is the invisible, spiritual world. Like Plotinus, the Sufis assumed the supremacy of the supernatural over the material world. It was by ascending from the visible realm to the spiritual that one might attain perfection, or union with the divinity. The key watchword in this philosophy was evolution: "There shall be no impassable gulf dividing God from man, spirit from matter: they shall be the first and last links of a single chain."[15]

In Sufi belief the first things which issued forth were the primal elements, called by some the objects of primary intellect. In this way also intelligences, souls, elements, the heavens, and the stars emerged. Then from these simple natures the vegetable, animal, and mineral kingdoms developed. The final end and aim of all was man, who, by a process of evolution, at last came forth.[16]

Jalal-ud-din Rumi (d.1273), the great Sufi teacher, in his immortal book *Masnawi*, gives a clear account of the Sufis' idea of evolution. The doctrines he enunciates stem directly from Greek ideas and anticipate by many centuries the Darwinian theory of evolution. The following lines are recognized as the central theme of Rumi's work:

> I died as mineral and became a plant,
> I died as plant and rose to animal,
> I died as animal and I was man.
> Why should I fear? When was I less by dying?
> Yet once more I shall die as man, to soar
> With angels blest; but even from angelhood
> I must pass on: all except God doth perish.
> When I have sacrificed my angel soul,
> I shall become what no mind e'er conceived,
> Oh, let me not exist! For Non-existence
> Proclaims in organ tones, 'To Him we shall return.'[17]

Shabastari, in a similar passage, describes man's journey from the lowest point, through the vegetative, animal, and human states up to the highest essence—obliteration of all consciousness and total perception of the world of external phenomena:

> Know first how the perfect man is produced

From the time he is first engendered.
He is produced at first as inanimate matter.
Next by the added spirit he is made sentient,
And acquires the motive powers from the Almighty.
Next he is made lord of will by "The Truth,"
There is no other final cause beyond man.
It is disclosed in man's own self.[18]

Ibn-i-Yamin, the famous Sufi poet of the fourteenth century, also refers to the evolution of man:

From the void of nonexistence to this dwelling-house of clay
I came, and rose from stone to plant; but that hath passed
    away.
Thereafter, through the working of the spirit's toil and
    strife,
I gained, but soon abandoned, some lowly form of life:
That too hath passed away.

In a human breast, no longer a mere unheeding brute,
This tiny drop of Being to a pearl I did transmute:
        That too hath passed away!
At the Holy Temple next did I foregather with the throng
    of angels, compassed it about, and gazed upon it long:
        That too hath passed away!
Forsaking Ibn-i-Yamin and from this to soaring free,
I abandoned all beside Him, so that naught was left.
    All else hath passed away.[19]

Man is complete only when he has gained intelligence.
This is the beginning and the end, and it makes the mystic
circle complete. From God is the origin and to God is the
return.[20]

Rumi, referring to the aim and object of our life, says:
"From realms of formlessness existence doth take form,
and fades again therein." He calls this the "procession of
essence into essence." The heart of the Sufi is inevitably
viewed as the mirror of the universe. After achieving intel-

ligence man must know truth. In order to know the truth or
to know God, man must look into his own heart.

Therefore, in Sufism, knowledge of oneself is an indis-
pensable preliminary to a knowledge of God. The contemplative life is dominated by these two realities: "Thou and
I"—"The lover and the beloved"—"God and the Soul."
Sadi of Shiraz (d.1292) is emphatic when he says, "I for God
and God for me, and no world beside."

5

The introduction of the idea of gnosis into Islamic and
Persian literature is the result of Sufi influence. The Sufi
distinguished three organs of communication: the heart
(*Del*) which knows Allah; the spirit (*Ruh*) which loves Him;
and the inmost ground of the soul (*Sirr*), which con-
templates Him. The nature of the heart, however, is considered perceptive rather than emotional, for whereas the
intellect cannot gain real knowledge of God, the heart is
capable of knowing the essence of all things, and when
illuminated by faith and knowledge it reflects the whole
content of the divine mind. God, according to the Qoran,
said, "My earth and my Heavens contain me not, but the
heart of my faithful servant contains me." He who truly
knows himself knows God. (*Man Arafah Nafseh Faquad Ar-
rafa Rabbeh.*)[21]

Rumi explains this point of view:

> The man of God is made wise by the truth,
> The man of God is not learned from the book,
> The man of God is beyond infidelity and faith,
> To the man of God right and wrong are alike.[22]

While ordinary knowledge (*Ilm*) is obtained by study and
hard work, mystic knowledge—*Marifat* (gnosis)—

according to the Sufis, is based on revelation or apocalyptic vision. It is not the result of any mental process, but is brought to realization through the influence of the divine upon the human. The influence, called *Faiz* or grace, flows down from God each moment, calling forth the soul and attracting it to Himself. Union, then, means receiving these emanations into oneself and being drawn more and more into the system expressed by Rumi:

The motion of every atom is towards its origin,
A man comes to be the thing on which he is bent,
The soul and the heart, by the attraction of wish and desire,
Assume the qualities of the Beloved.[23]

Those who seek truth, according to Sufis, are of three types:

1. The worshippers to whom God will make Himself known by means of reward. They worship Him in the hope of winning paradise.

2. The philosophers and scholastic theologians to whom God will make Himself known by means of glory. Yet, they can never find the glorious God whom they seek; wherefore they assert that his essence is unknowable.

3. The gnostics, to whom God will make Himself known by means of ecstasy. They are possessed and controlled by a rapture that deprives them of the consciousness of individual existence.

The gnostic performs only such acts of worship as are in accordance with his vision of God, though in so doing he necessarily disobeys the religious law made for ordinary people. His inward feeling must determine how valid the external forms of religion are, nor need he be dismayed if his inner experience conflicts with the religious institutions, rules, and rituals. Institutions of religion regard separate things, but gnosis perceives the all-embracing unity.[24]

According to Dhul Nun, the father of Muslim theosophy, the gnostics "move as God causes them to move, and their words are the words of God which roll upon their tongue, and their sight is the sight of God which has entered their eyes."[25]

Man is complete when he has gained gnosis, but gnosis is also the primal element; so it is the beginning and the end, the first and the last, and through it the mystic circle is perfect. Rumi, referring to the supreme cycle, states:

From realms of formlessness, existence doth take form,
And fades again therein, to him we must return.[26]

Sufis believe that man has the privilege of possessing divine attributes. According to the Qoran, God proferred a deposit of divine attributes to the heavens and to the earth and to the mountains between them, but when they refused He entrusted them to man. So it is that the universe is the mirror of God, as the heart of man is the mirror of the universe. The man who is seeking God or the truth must look into his heart.

Jami, a great Sufi teacher (d. 1492), gives us a Sufi interpretation of gnosis and God's manifestation in the human heart in the following verses:

From all eternity the Beloved unveiled this beauty in the solitude of the unseen,

He held up the mirror to his own face, He displayed His loveliness to himself;

He was both the spectator and the spectacle, no eye but His had surveyed the universe.

All was one, there was no duality, no pretense of "mine" or "thine."

The vast orb of Heaven, with its myriad incomings and outgoings, was concealed in a single point.

The creation lay cradled in the sleep of nonexistence, like a child ere it has breathed.

The love of the Beloved, seeing what was not, regarded nonentity as existent.

Although he beheld his attributes and qualities as a perfect whole in his own essence,

Yet he desired that they should be displayed to him in another mirror,

And that each one of his eternal attributes should become manifest accordingly in a diverse form.

Therefore He created the verdant fields of time and space and the life-giving gardens of the world,

That every branch and leaf and fruit might show forth His various perfection.

The cypress gave a hint of His comely stature, the rose gave tidings of His beauteous countenance.

Wherever beauty peeped out, love appeared beside it, Whenever beauty shone in a rosy cheek, love lit His torch from the flame.

Whenever beauty dwelt in dark tresses, love came and found a heart entangled in their coils.

Beauty and love are as body and soul; beauty is the mind and love the precious stone.

They have always been together from the very first Never have they travelled but in each other's company.

Man is the crown and final cause of the universe.[27]

Though man is last in order of creation, he is first in the process of divine thought, for the essential part of man is the primal intelligence of universal reason which emanated immediately from the god-head. The gnostic is "a copy made in the image of God." Gnosis, therefore, is unification, realization of the fact that one has achieved the last stages of a mystical journey and has become the "man of God."

Man, then, occupies a central place in the Sufi doctrine. Thus, it is the primary function of man to reveal and realize his divine nature, and the perfect man can represent all the attributes of God:

> The function of the human rational soul is the noblest function of all, for it is itself the noblest of spirits. Its function consists of reflecting upon things of art and meditating upon things of beauty: its gaze being turned towards the higher world, it loves not this lower abode and meaner station. Belonging as man's soul does to the higher side of life and to the primal substance . . . its function is to wait for the revelation of truths. . . . It is distinguished from other spirits by the possessing of perfect reason and far-reaching, all-embracing thought; its ambition and striving all through life is to purify the sensual impressions and to perceive the world of intelligible truths.[28]

Man received the most noble of forms, and his human material was formed with the finest traits that adorn the living creature. God blessed this work with the gift of His own Holy Spirit and endowed man with the powers of intellect and speech, so that he possessed the attributes of his own Creator. These precious gifts were bestowed upon him, so as to enable him to comprehend the wondrous works of his Divine Originator and to speak His praise. Man was gifted with a mental capacity in order to attain the

brotherhood of races and religions and to dedicate his life
to serving his fellow men:

> The moment man to this low world was given,
> A ladder stood whereby thou might aspire;
> And first thy steps, which upward still have striven.
> From mineral mounted to the plant, then higher
> To animal existence: next, the man,
> With the knowledge, reason, faith. O wondrous goal!
> This body, which a crumb of dust began—
> How fairly fashioned the consummate whole!
> Yet stay not here thy journey; thou shalt grow
> An angel bright and home far off in heaven.
> Plod on, plunge last in the great sea, that so
> Thy little drop make oceans seven times seven.[29]

The stages of the Mystical Journey are eight in number:
service, love, abstention, knowledge, ecstasy, truth, union,
self-negation. It is very difficult to analyze all the words of
the Sufi poets or to say to which stages of gnosis they refer,
but these stages are invariably present, though not necessarily in any systematic order. Generally speaking, the stage of
love is the most popular subject of the Sufi poets who sing of
God and man as the Beloved and the Lover.

6

The most influential aspect of Sufism was its doctrine of
universalism and world brotherhood, and its root can be
found in both ancient Persian culture and in the Qoran:
1. The Persians were Aryan in language, but their culture was universal; and they served historically as conveyers
to future civilizations which would flourish in the Mediter-
ranean area.
Cyrus the Great was the first enlightened king to forge
the heterogeneous nations he had conquered into a unified

empire through the exercise of tolerance and cultural freedom. He viewed all gods and religions as equal. Under his
benevolent rule art flourished and different ideas and religions were freely practiced. He prohibited the killing of prisoners, outlawed slavery, and proclaimed that all exiled
peoples in his vast realm, including the Jews, would be
permitted to return to their respective homelands if they
wished. His generosity was praised in the grandiloquent
words of Isaiah: "Thus says the Lord to his anointed, to
Cyrus, whose right hand I have grasped. He shall build my
city and set my exiles free."[30]

Another Jewish leader, Ezra, was a scribe in the court of
the Persian King Artaxerxes in Susa. When the King heard
of the sad plight of the Jews in Jerusalem he ordered Ezra
to organize a second Zionade which proved successful beyond all expectations of the Jewish leaders. Later on, King
Artaxerxes appointed Nehemiah as governor of Jerusalem.
The team of Ezra and Nehemiah, with the King's financial
help and military aid, fortified Jerusalem and protected the
Jewish people against their enemies. This Persian tolerance
of and respect for freedom of religion and culture was responsible for the praise and exaltation showered on Cyrus
and his successors by Ezra, Isaiah, and Daniel.

2. Muhammad connected his mission with the teachings
of all the prophets of Israel and of Christ. He announced
that the Holy Kaaba had been consecrated by Abraham. He
went so far as to obscure the differences of race and color
by extending the memories of his people back to the day of
creation and gave the Muslims a universal tradition based
on the holy scriptures of the Zoroastrians, Jews, and Christians.

The principle of the brotherhood and universalism of
man laid down in the Qoran is very broad. Muhammad
clearly states: "The believers should never let one group

laugh at the other groups because they may be better than you. Do not allow women to laugh at other women. Do not find fault with your fellow man and do not call them names. Avoid suspicion, for suspicion is in some cases sin. Do not spy on others; avoid backbiting.

"Oh you people of the world: we have created you of a male and a female, and we made you into clans and tribes that you may know each other. Surely the most respected men in the eyes of God are those who are most virtuous. Surely God is well aware."[31]

The above verse in the Qoran is not addressed to Arabs or Muslims but to all the people of the world as members of a family equal in the eyes of their Creator. Their divisions into nations, tribes and families should not result in religious, racial, national, or social prejudices. Superiority in this universal world, according to the Qoran, does not depend on family, wealth, rank, title, creed or color, but on virtue, love, and moral integrity. Virtue and love must always be put before glory and ambition. Glory in this world is the shadow of virtue. Therefore, virtue and love must be the cornerstone of the edifice of our society. Whoever abandons virtue and love ends up with a bare and miserable life which "only resembles that of the brute beasts that follow headlong their appetite which to them is their only law."

7

In Ibni Arabi (born in Spain in A.D. 1165), we find an elaboration of the doctrine of pantheism and the idea of the "perfect man."[32] The fundamental principle of his system is the Unity of Being: "There is no real difference between the Essence and its attributes or, in other words, between God and the Universe." Arabi's pantheistic philosophy strengthens the Islamic doctrine of the "perfect man," created in the image of God (*Al Insan al Kamel*). Only through this "perfect man" does God know Himself and make Himself known. He is the eye of the world whereby God sees His own works.[33]

Many Islamic leaders were shocked by the so-called blasphemous expressions which appeared in his writings. His doctrine of the incarnation of God in man (*Hulul*) and the identification of man with God was labeled heretical and was violently condemned.

Arabi's doctrine was a combination of Manichean, Gnostic, Neoplatonic and Christian speculations, which he tried to relate to the teachings of the prophet Muhammad. He calls Muhammad "the idea of ideas," the mediator, the vice-regent of God, the God-man who has descended to this earthly sphere to make manifest the glory of Him who brought the Universe into existence.

The importance of Ibn Arabi's philosophy lay in its transcendence of the bounds of doctrinal religion. If God is the "self" of all things sensible and intelligible, it follows that He reveals Himself to every form of belief:

> The believer praises the God who is in his form of belief and with whom he has connected himself. He praises none but himself, for his God is made by himself. For this reason he blames the beliefs of others, which he would not do, if he were just. Beyond doubt, the worshipper of this particular God shows ignorance when he criticizes others on account of their beliefs. God said, 'I am in My servant's opinion of Me, I do not manifest Myself to him save in the form of his belief.' God is absolute or restricted, as He pleases; and the God of religious belief is subject to limitations, for He is the God who is contained in the hearts of His servant.
>
> • • • • •
>
> My heart is capable of every form:
> A cloister for the monk, a fane for idols,
> A pasture for gazelles, the votary's Kaba,

The tables of the Torah, the Koran.
Love is the faith I hold: wherever I turn
His camels, still the one true faith is mine.[34]

8

Central to Sufism is the belief that all the evil thoughts
which breed dislike, hatred and division must be cast aside.
Indifference to all doctrinal distinctions has become a cardinal Sufi dogma:

While my loved phantom dwells in pagoda's bounds
'Twere mortal sin, should I the Kaaba compass round,
The Kaaba is but a church, if there His trace be lost;
The church my only Kaaba, while He there is found.

Omar Khayyam, describing this universalism, wrote:

In cell and cloister, monastery and synagogue, one lies
In dread of Hell, one dreams of paradise.
But none that know the secrets of the Lord
Have sown their hearts with such like fantasies.

Being tired of the cruelties and crimes committed in the
name of religion, Hafiz shouted: "If Islam be that which
Hafiz practices, alas if there should be a day of judgment!"
On another occasion Hafiz shows his contempt for the
fanaticism and narrow-mindedness of his time:

What care if sober or drunk, every man is seeking the
Friend;
What care if in Mosque or Church, each place is the house
of love,
What care if in Hell or Heaven we alight, if the Friend be
there?
What care if in Mosque or Church we kneel, if our prayer
be true?

Reacting with sobriety and serenity to the disturbing events and conflicts of his time, Hafiz demonstrated a great spiritual strength in believing that soon clashes and conflicts, struggles and strife, the hypocrisy and demagoguery of the clergy would give their place to a world of brotherhood, unity and stability, dominated by universal ideals:

O will it be that they will reopen the doors of the taverns,
And will loosen the knots from our tangled affairs?
Cut the strings of the harp in mourning for the death of
    pure wine,
So that all of the magician's children may loosen their
    curled locks,
Write the letter of condolence for the disappearance of
    wine,
So that all the comrades may let loose tears from their
    eyelashes.
They have closed the doors of the wine-taverns; O God
    suffer not
That they should open the doors of the house of deceit and
    hypocrisy.
If they have closed them for the sake of demagogues and
    the self-righteous zealot
Be of good heart, for they will reopen them for God's
    sake.[35]

When mysticism is fully realized, it leads the Sufi to the annihilation of self in the absolute truth; he becomes a friend of God, a servant to His people, and a perfect man:

When preaching unity with unitarian pen,
Blot out and cancel every page that tells of selfishness of
    men.[36]

Jami, the Sufi mentor, refers to true Sufis:

Wouldst thou thyself from selfhood disembroil,

To banish vain desire must be thy toil,
Empty thy hand of all it closes on,
And suffer many a blow and not recoil.

The Sufi argues that the ordinary theologian of any creed is in the bondage of vested interest and is enslaved to the dogma of his religion, believing blindly what the establishment requires him to believe. But the Sufi, who has no other interest but his love of God and world brotherhood, gains his knowledge and his strength by direct and personal communication with his Creator. Hassan of Basra states: "An ounce of genuine decency is better than a thousand times of fasting and prayers."[37]

"The keynote of Sufism," according to Reynold Nicholson, "is disinterested, selfless devotion, in a word, love. The whole of Sufism is a protest against the unnatural divorce between God and man."[38]

9

Abu Said Ibn Abul Khair (A.D. 967–1049) is described by his biographers as the master of theosophic verse and the first to popularize the quatrain and to make it the focus of all mystic pantheistic ideas: "I went from God to God until they cried from me in me, O Thou God. Nothing is better for man than to be without aught, having no asceticism, no theory, no practice. When he is without all, he is with all. I am the wine-drinker and the wine and the cup-bearer. Verily I am God, there is no God except me, so worship me."[39]

The following quatrains are a few specimens of Abu Said's sayings. They serve to show that "if the theosophical basis of Sufism is distinctly Greek, its mystical extravagances are no less distinctively Oriental."

Said I, 'to whom belongs thy beauty?'
He replied, 'since I alone exist, to Me;

Lover, Beloved and Love am I in one,
Beauty, and Mirror, and the Eyes which see.

'Those men who lavish on me titles fair
Know not my heart, nor what is hidden there;
But if they once could turn me inside out,
They'd doom me to the burning, that I'll swear.

'The gnostic, who hath known the mystery,
Is one with God, and from his selfhood free:
Affirm God's being and deny thine own:
This is the meaning of *no God but He*.

'My countenance is blanched of Islam hue;
More honour to infidels' dog is due.
So black with shame's my visage that of me
Hell is ashamed, and Hell's despairing crew.

'When me at length thy love's embrace shall claim
To glance at paradise I'd deem it shame,
While to a Thee-less Heaven were I called,
Such Heaven and Hell to me would seem the same.

'To gladden one poor heart of man is more,
Be sure, than fanes a thousand to restore:
And one free man by kindness to enslave
Is better than to free of slaves a score.

'Till mosque and seminary fall beneath ruin's ban
And doubt and faith be interchanged in man,
How can the order of the Sufi
Prevail, and raise up one true Musalman?'[40]

Rumi states that love is the guide and uniting force of Sufism from beginning to end. The outward rituals in churches, mosques, temples and pagodas are void of any reality, and are the cause of all prejudices, hatred and strife:

Cross and Christians, from end to end
I surveyed, He was not on the cross.

I went to the idol temple, to the ancient pagoda
No trace was visible there.
I bent the reins of search to the Kaaba,
He was not in that resort of old and young,
I gazed into my own heart;
There I saw him, he was nowhere else.
In the whirl of its transport my spirit was tossed,
Till each atom of separate being I lost.

Say not that all these creeds are false,
The false ones capture hearts by the scent of truth
Say not they are all erroneous thoughts,
There is thought in the world void of reality.
He who says everything is true is a fool,
He who says all is false is a knave.[41]

Because the Sufis abandoned external form and rituals
and sang the praise of universal truth which is within the
reach of everybody regardless of creed, color, or national-
ity, Sufism became a religion which was both international
and universal. Its literature and ideas have had a wide audience in North Africa, India, Malaya, China, and Indonesia.

In Eternity without beginning the radiancy of thy beauty
    gloried in its own splendour;
Love was revealed and its fire set the world aflame.

Reason desired to kindle its lamp from that flame of Thy
    love,
The lightning of jealousy flashed, and the world was thrown
    into confusion.

Others staked their fortune on ease and would not take up
    the burden of Love;
We, Thy lovers, were the ones whose hearts, experienced in
    grief, staked all on grief and took up the burden of Love.

He, God, looked forth and beheld His own form in the
    world, in the person of Adam;

He pitched His tent in the field of Adam's body, which He
    had formed of water and clay.

Hafiz wrote in his joy-book of Love-for-Thee on the day
    when his pen denounced all desire for the goods of this
    world, renounced happiness in what the world can
    offer.[42]

Ubayd-i-Zakani, the prominent satirical poet of the fourteenth century, takes to task both spiritual and temporal
leaders of his time for their lack of honesty and integrity,
and their narrow-mindedness: He calls them horrible hacks
and hustlers. He advises people to ignore the self-righteous
and hypocritical preachings of the church and judge a man
not by his social status or religious affiliation but by his
virtues and nobility:

Of whatever creed thou are, be magnanimous and gener-
    ous,
For infidelity combined with virtue is better than
Islam combined with dishonesty and immorality.
Whether or not a prophet comes between virtuous in con-
    duct,
For he whose conduct is virtuous will not go to Hell.

Sadi of Shiraz, who is praised by Emerson and called "the
poet of friendship, love, self-devotion and serenity," asserts
the morality of the Sufi ideal of the brotherhood of man in
the following verse:

> The sons of men are members
> In a body whole related,
> For of a single essence
> Are they each and all created,
> When fortune persecutes with pain
> One member sorely, surely
> The other members of the body

Cannot stand securely.
O you who from another's troubles
Turn aside your view,
It is not fitting they bestow
The name of "man" on you.

10

The Sufis take great issue with the idea that God is arbitrary, vengeful, and awesome. They try to be rational and concerned with the illumination of reason. They base their lives upon the fact that they live with God and God with them. They speak of and believe in God as the center and goal of all that exists. This God is all-compassionate and all-merciful:

The sinner's bleeding heart in anguish sighs,
The saint upon his piety relies,
Doth he not know that God resisteth pride,
But takes the low in spirit to His side?
Whose heart is vile, but outside fair to see,
For him hell's gates yawn wide, he wants no key,
Humility in His sight is more meet
Than strict religious forms and self-conceit.
Thy self-esteem but proves how bad thou art,
For egotism with God can have no part;
Boast not thyself—however swift his pace,
Not every skillful rider wins the race,
Wise men have left for all this saying true,
And Sadi in this tale remindeth you,
The sinner penitent hath less to fear
Than he whose piety is not sincere.[43]

11

Another Sufi contribution was the reconciliation of speculative thought with religious revelations. Although the Sufis borrowed from every philosophy and creed, their ideas of universalism, harmony, world brotherhood, God, man, and nature deviate widely from the teachings of the religious institutions. Their doctrine of monotheistic mysticism teaches that the human mind is capable through intuition and reasoning of apprehending God's existence and of cleansing man's heart of hatred, prejudice, and animosity.

They were the first to outline a psychology of faith and to reconcile all religions which, according to them, conflicted with one another only in appearance. They tried to synthesize Greek philosophy and the Semitic religions and constantly strove to eliminate ideological differences. No religion turns us away from the truth. Philosophy seeks it, prophets explain it, theology confuses, but mysticism finds truth in every philosophy, idea, and religion. The truth is that God is the fullest plenitude of being, representing all, undivided unity, the most perfect God and the all-merciful. What disturbs this universalism and the peace of unity is personal ambition and the vanity of those who see themselves as God's public relations representatives. In this way the Sufis created a spiritual environment unknown in Greek philosophy or in churches and temples.

They even dared to speak about the nature of the Deity. "The nature of God," according to the Sufis, "is an infinite and illimitable light, a boundless and fathomless ocean, compared with which the entire universe is more insignificant than a drop of water in the sea. God is always near to all men but men are always far from God because they are not aware of His proximity. The beautiful truth is that He is ever near to those who seek Him, regardless of their creed or their belief."[44]

The following verses explain Sufi beliefs about the unity of God and the universality of belief:

The lamps are different, but the light is the same: it comes from beyond.

If thou keep looking at the lamp, thou art lost: for thence
arises the appearance of number and plurality.
Fix thy gaze upon the light, and thou art delivered from the
dualism inherent in the finite body.
O thou who art the kernel of Existence, the disagreement
between Muslims, Zoroastrian, Christians and Jews depends on the standpoint.
Some Hindus brought an elephant, which they exhibited in
a dark shed.
As seeing it with the eye was impossible, everyone felt it with
the palm of his hand.
The hand of one fell on its trunk: he said, "This animal is
like a water-pipe."
Another touched its ear: to him the creature seemed like a
fan.
Another handled its leg and described the elephant as having the shape of a pillar.
Another stroked its back. "Truly," said he, "this elephant
resembles a throne."
Had each of them held a lighted candle, there would have
been no contradiction in their words.[45]

We all err—Muslims, Christians, Jews, and Magicians;
Two make Humanity's universal sect;
One man intelligent without religion,
And one religious without intellect.[46]

Sufi literature in both its form and content bears the
stamp of freshness, charm, and catholicity. Sufi poets often
dared not say what they meant, but they said enough to
show that in their view not authority and tradition, but
reason and conscience, must decide whether actions are
right or wrong and whether beliefs are true or false. They
apply a rationalistic standard to all revealed religions, not
excepting Islam.

Ecumenism, mysticism, unity of man with God, pantheism, and universal brotherhood—all Sufi doctrines—
are enunciated in this hymn, by Shabastari, to the ultimate glory of God:

All sects but multiply the I and Thou:
This I and Thou belong to partial being;
When I and Thou and several beings vanish,
Then mosque and church shall bind these never more,
Our individual life is but a phantom:
Make clear thine eye, and see reality!
Go, man! with Moses to the wilderness,
And hear with him that voice 'I am the Lord!'
While, like a mountain that shuts out the sun,
Thine eye lifts up its head, thou shalt not see me,
The lightning strikes the mountain into ruins
And o'er the levelled dust the glory leaps.[47]

There is a deep fatalistic streak in Sufism. Some of the most well-known lines written about the inevitability of fate are those of Omar Khayyam:

LXXI
The Moving Finger writes; and, having writ,
Moves on: nor all of your Piety nor Wit
Shall lure it back to cancel half a Line,
Nor all your Tears wash out a Word of it.[48]

Still another verse, this by Rumi, illustrates this fatalistic doctrine:

We are the flute, our music is all Thine;
We are the mountain echoing only Thee
Pieces of chess Thou marshallest in line
And move to defeat or victory;
Lions emblazoned high on flags unfurled
Thy wind invisible sweeps us through the world.[49]

Sadi, too, believed that:

He whom the turning world is to afflict
Will be guided by the times against his aim.
A pigeon destined not to see its nest again
Will be carried by fate towards the grain and net.[50]

Yet there is some contradiction between the Sufis' belief, on the one hand, in fate and their emphasis, on the other hand, on hard work, free will, and faith in sincere effort. Sadi, himself, wrote:

Although daily food may come unawares
It is wise to seek it all over the world
And although no one dies without the decree of fate
Thou must not rush into the jaws of a dragon.[51]

Rumi, too, stresses the need for making efforts based on faith and hope:

When you put a cargo on board a ship, you make that
    venture on trust,
For you know not whether you will be drowned or come
    safe to land.
If you say, "I will not embark till I am certain of my fate,"
Then you will do no trade: the secret of these two destinies
    is never disclosed.
The faint-hearted merchant neither gains nor loses; nay, he
    loses: one must take fire in order to get light.
Since all affairs turn upon hope, surely faith is the best
    object of hope, for thereby you win salvation.[52]

The contradiction, then, is not an insoluble one: According to the Sufis, fate determines our circumstances, but we must choose to react or not to react to them. Fate may impel, but it does not compel us to sit back and await our destiny; rather it is action, based upon hope and faith, that redeems us.

In summary the reader will perceive that Sufism is a word uniting many divergent meanings, and does not represent any particular religion or dogmas exclusively. Sufism is not a creed; it has no dogmatic systems; the "ways" by which one seeks God "are as numerous as the number of the people of the world."

"The essence of Sufism," according to Reynold A. Nicholson, "is its extreme type, which is pantheistic and speculative rather than ascetic and devotional. Strange as it may seem to our Western egoism, the prospect of sharing in the general, impersonal immortality of human soul kindled in Sufis an enthusiasm as deep and triumphant as that of the most ardent believer in personal life continuing beyond the grave."[53] Rumi, after describing the evolution of man in the material world and anticipating his further growth in the spiritual universe, utters a heart-felt prayer for what? For self-annihilation in the ocean of the Godhead."

God hath not created in the earth or in the lofty heaven anything more occult than the spirit of Man.
He hath revealed the mystery of all things, moist and dry, but He hath sealed the mystery of the spirit: "it is of the Word of my Lord."
Since the august eye of the Witness beheld that spirit, naught remains hidden from him.
God is named "the Just," and the Witness belongs to Him: the just Witness is the eye of the Beloved.
The object of God's Regard in both worlds is the pure heart: the King's gaze is fixed upon the favourite.
The mystery of His amorous play with His favourite was the origin of all the veils which He hath made.
Hence our Loving Lord said to the Prophet on the night of the Ascension: "But for thee I would not have created the heavens."[54]

1. *Hujwiri*, translated by Grunebaum, op. cit., p. 382.
2. *Abu Naim*, Hily IX, p. 342, translated by A. J. Arberry.
3. *Ibid.*, pp. 53–54.
4. Shabastari, Mahmud; *Gulshan* Raz, translated by E. H. Whinfield, London, 1880, Trubner and Co., p. 44.
5. See Attar, Farid ud-din; *Muslim Saints and Mystics*, translated, by A. J. Arberry, London, Routledge and Kegan Paul, 1966, pp. 100–22.
6. *Ibid.*
7. A. J. Arberry (ed.), *The Legacy of Persia*, The Clarendon Press, Oxford, 1953, pp. 159–60.

8. Wickens, G. M., *The Legacy of Persia*, pp. 160–63.
9. Rice, Cyprian, *The Persian Sufis*, London, George Allen and Unwin, p. 11.
10. Attar, *op. cit.*, translated by Reynold A. Nicholson, p. 186.
11. R. A. Nicholson, *The Idea of Personality in Sufism*, Cambridge University Press, 1923, p. 30.
12. *Ibid.*
13. R. A. Nicholson, *Legacy of Islam*, p. 217.
14. Wickens, *op. cit.*, p. 162.
15. E. Sell, *Essays on Islam*, Madras, 1901: S.P.C.K. Depot, p. 10.
16. *Ibid.*
17. Nicholson, R. A., *Mystic of Islam*, George Bell & Sons, Ltd., London, 1914, p. 164.
18. Shabastari, *op. cit.*, p. 33.
19. Brown, E. G., *A Literary History of Persia*, vol. III, pp. 216–17.
20. Sell, *op. cit.*, p. 12.
21. R. A. Nicholson, *The Mysticism of Islam*, London, Routledge, 1963, pp. 70–71.
22. Rumi, *Divan* Shamsi Tabriz.
23. *Ibid.*
24. Miffari, *Treatise on Speculative Mysticism*, quoted by Nicholson, *op. cit.*, pp. 71–72.
25. *Ibid.*, p. 73.
26. Rumi, *Masnawi*, Book 1, Tale 5, p. 364, translated by G. E. Sell.
27. Nicholson, *op. cit.*, p. 82.
28. Avicenna (ibn-Sina), d. A.D. 1037, translated by A. J. Arberry.
29. *Rumi, op. cit.*
30. Isaiah 45:1, 13.
31. Qoran, XLIX: 11, 12, 13.
32. Arabi rejected all authority (*Taglid*). "I am not one of those who say, 'Ibn Hazm said so and so'; I am an adherent of the sacred law." He considered himself as divinely illuminated and infallible.
33. Nicholson, *A Literary History of Arabs, op. cit.*, p. 401.
34. Nicholson, Reynold A., *Translations of Eastern Poetry and Prose*, London, Cambridge University Press, 1922, p. 148.
35. Hafiz, *Divan*, translated by G. Bell.
36. Hafiz, *Divan*, quoted by Sell, *op. cit.*, p. 18.
37. Qushyri, *Risalatul Quslayryya* (Tracts of Qushayry, A.D. 1074) Edition 1909, p. 63.
38. Nicholson, *A Literary History of The Arabs, op. cit.*, p. 231.
39. *Ibid.*, p. 391.
40. E. G. Browne, *A History of Persian Literature*, vol. II, T. Fisher Unwin, London, pp. 261–67.
41. Rumi, translated by R. A. Nicholson, Cambridge University Press, 1898, p. 20.
42. Hafiz, translated by the authors.
43. Sadi, *Divan*, p. 68.
44. Nafasi, a Sufi mentor who lived in the thirteenth century, translated by H. E. Palmer.
45. R. A. Nicholson, *Rumi, Poet and Mystic* (1207–75), George Allen & Unwin Ltd., London, p. 166.
46. Maarry, *Meditations*, translated by R. A. Nicholson, pp. 102–07.
47. *Shabastari*, translated by R. A. Vaughan, pp. 43, 44.
48. From "The Rubáiyát of Omar Khayyám," translated by Edward FitzGerald.
49. Rumi, *Divan*, translated by R. A. Nicholson, p. 127.

50. Sadi, *Gulistan,* p. 167.
51. *Ibid.*
52. Rumi, *op. cit.*
53. Nicholson, *Mystic of Islam,* George Bell & Sons, Ltd., London, 1914.
54. Nicholson, R. A., *Rumi, Poet and Mystic,* George Allen & Unwin Ltd., London, 1950, p. 127.

4
Al-Ghazzali, the Mind of Sufism

The heart which stands aloof from pain and woe
No seal or signature of Love can show:
Thy Love, thy Love I chose, and as for wealth,
If wealth be not my portion, be it so!
For wealth, I ween, pertaineth to the World;
Ne'er can the World and Love together go!
So long as Thou dost dwell within my heart
Ne'er can my heart become the thrall of Woe.

In presenting the Sufi thinkers we start with al-Ghazzali, not
only because he is probably the greatest Islamic theologian,
philosopher, teacher, and mystic, but also because he represents the best in the intellectual and humanitarian firma-
ment of the eleventh century. Al-Ghazzali is the singular
representative of Persian character, Sufi doctrine, and Islamic culture. Like Buddha, al-Ghazzali abandoned worldly
success when it conflicted with his conscience, and like St.
Thomas he strove to reconcile reason and revelation. He is
remarkable not for innovations or originality, "but for the
qualities of piety, charity, humility, common sense, love of
his fellow men, and the objectivity which he brought to the

75

study of philosophy and to the practice of mysticism."¹
When to these qualities are added profound learning and a
clearly attractive personality, he will readily be seen to be a
very rare and precious ornament to Islam, as he would be to
any faith. "He came as near as anyone ever did to reconcil-
ing Islam's inner contradictions and to relieving its external
stresses; that his success in this respect is not to be compared with the results achieved by St. Thomas Aquinas on
the Christian side is probably attributable less to any inferiority on his part than to the very nature of these difficulties in Islam."²

Al-Ghazzali has been acclaimed in both the Islamic and
Christian worlds as the best representative of the universal
mind. His reputation rests on the fact that he tried to reconcile Islam with Greek philosophy and the fundamentals of
other religions. In this attempt he humanized Muslim
theology and at the same time saved it from being either
diluted or destroyed by Neo-Platonism. He also tried to
show to orthodoxy the beauty of Sufism and he endlessly
attempted to bring about a close contact between the two,
although orthodox theologians nevertheless went their own
way, as did the Sufis. The personality and moral power of
al-Ghazzali, however, became a major source of inspiration
for Sufis, and his prestige forced the Orthodox theologians
to show more respect for dissenters.

2

Abu-Hamid Muhammad al-Ghazzali was born in 1058 at
Tous, in the northeastern part of Persia. This district was
the center of the Islamic intellectual world and the birthplace of a large number of religious teachers, poets, Sufi
preachers, writers, and scientists. In A.D. 1072 it came
under the Rule of Malik Shah and his great Vizier (Chancel-

lor) Nizam ul Mulk. Under the latter's patronage a circle of most distinguished scholars collected at the court while others taught at the colleges and universities at Balkh, Samarkand, Merv, Nishapour, Herat, Isfahan, Amul, Basra, Mosul, Baghdad, and Rey.

Al-Ghazzali's education became the responsibility of a well-known Sufi teacher. It was with the thought of what he owed to this great teacher that al-Ghazzali wrote years later: "Let the student be assured that more is due to the teacher than the father, for the teacher is the cause to him of eternal life and the father the cause only of his temporal life. It was for that reason that Alexander, when asked whether he honored his teacher or his father the more, replied, 'My teacher most certainly.' "[3] His thesis on the right conduct of the student towards his mentor could be instructive to students of any generation: "A student should seek learning for the sake of knowledge. He should not use it for anything except in the service of God and man. He should always show respect for his teacher, should not pester him when he is tired, should listen attentively, should not speak rudely. A student should not criticize his teacher for his appearance or outward conduct, even if he thinks it inappropriate, since the teacher is well aware of what he is doing and he must have a reason of which the student is not aware."[4]

In 1091, Nizam al Mulk appointed al-Ghazzali to the Chair of Philosophy and Theology at Nizamyeh University in Baghdad—an exceptional honor for a man who was only thirty-four years old. Baghdad, the capital of the Abbasside Caliphs, was at this time at the height of its wealth, culture, and learning. As early as 830, Caliph al-Mamun had established the House of Wisdom as a center of learning, research, and translation of Indian, Persian, and Greek books into Arabic. When Al-Ghazzali started lecturing at

Nizamyeh, there were thirty-six libraries and several colleges (Madrassah) at Baghdad.

At Nizamyeh, not only theology and philosophy, but medicine and sciences were taught in an atmosphere of complete academic freedom to students from all parts of the Muslim world. Although al-Ghazzali was the youngest professor, he received the warmest welcome in Baghdad. He astonished all the wise men by the depth of his knowledge, the excellence of his delivery, his fluency of language, and the lucidity of his explanations. His lectures attracted savants and scholars from all over the Muslim Empire. Later, in addition to his professorship at Nizamyeh, he was appointed *Imam* of Iraq. In this position he was called upon to give legal interpretations of the canon law (*Fatwa*).

Yet in spite of his success, wealth, prestige, and honor, al-Ghazzali was not happy with what he saw in the capital of the Islamic Empire. He noticed that while the political and religious leaders were assiduous in certain useless practices of convention, they ignored their true responsibility to their own people. He became determined to "unveil the truth in its entirety." He started to question the practice of justice and to condemn the hypocrisy of the caliphs. Developing a horror for oppression and injustice, he warned his students not to accept tyrannical pomp and proud opulence with indifference but to show resistance and to destroy them. To pray, but to keep one's vices; to fast, but to hate; to conspire, to kill, to hurt and to persecute was not the way of salvation, but the road to destruction. The peace and happiness of all humanity was al-Ghazzali's wish. His time was no different from ours or from that of Voltaire who lamented:

This world is a great dance in which fools disguised under the laughable names . . . think to inflate their being and elevate their baseness. We are surprised in vain by the displays of vanity; all mortals are equal, their masks are different. Our five imperfect senses, given to us by nature, are the sole measure of our good and evil. Do kings have six? And are their souls and bodies of a different kind? Have they other springs? All are born from the same mud, they drag out their childhood in the same weakness; and the rich and the poor, and the weak and the strong all go on equally from sorrow to death.

At the height of his fame, al-Ghazzali decided to give away all his wealth, except a small amount necessary to maintain his family, and in 1096 he left Baghdad.[5] As he explains in his famous book, *The Faith and Practice of al-Ghazzali*: "I was burdened with the teaching and instruction of three hundred students in Baghdad. By my solitary studies God brought me to complete understanding of the science of philosophers."[6]

Having mastered all the sciences, and having maintained associations with the so-called great and learned men of his time, al-Ghazzali confessed: "It is customary with weaker intellects thus to take the man as criterion of the truth and not the truth as the criterion of the man. The intelligent man follows Ali, Muhammad's fourth successor, who said, 'Do not know the truth by the men, but know the truth, and then you will know who are truthful, *and that will make you free.*' "

It is prevalent among the majority of men, according to al-Ghazzali, that whenever one ascribes a statement to an author of whom he approves, he accepts it, even if it is false. On the other hand, whenever one ascribes a truth to an author of whom he disapproves, he rejects it at once. Men always make their favorite politician or writer the criterion of truth and not truth the criterion of their heroes. And that is exactly what is wrong with our world.

As a result of his disillusionment with his society and of

his long search for peace of mind he turned to Sufism. Referring to his change of heart, al-Ghazzali stated:

"I next turned with set purpose to the method of Sufism. I knew that the Sufi way includes both intellectual belief and practical activity; the latter consists in getting rid of the obstacles in the self and in stripping off its base characteristics and vicious morals, so that the heart may attain the freedom from what is not God and the constant recollection of him.

"The intellectual belief was easier. But it became clear to me, however, that what is most distinctive of mysticism is something which cannot be apprehended by study, but only by immediate experience (*Dhawg*—literally, 'tasting'), by ecstasy and by a moral change.

"I apprehended clearly that the mystics were men who had real experience, not men of words, and that I had already progressed as far as was possible by way of intellectual apprehension.

"It had already become clear to me that I had no hope of the bliss of the world to come save through a God-fearing life and the withdrawal of myself from vain desire."[7]

It was at this point that al-Ghazzali decided to abandon the mansion of deception and hypocrisy and to turn away from worldly position and material entanglements. He believed that men destroy themselves through avarice, ambition, and desire for power. They abandon decency, justice, and compassion because of their greed and lust. They steal, they deceive, they kill, and finally they destroy everything decent, including themselves. The Sufis believed that the noble truths which could change the world if they were properly understood were these: Suffering is universal. The cause of human suffering is greed and worldly desire. The elimination of desire and greed can cure the sickness of society. The Sufi way is designed to help man eliminate desire, hatred, and lust for power and possessions.

Al-Ghazzali believed that knowledge starts with "knowing thyself." Many Islamic sayings give the self special status in relation to God. "He who knows himself has known God" (*Man Arrefeh Nafsoh Faqad Arrefeh Rabboh*); "I have breathed into him (man) of my spirit;" "God created Adam in His own image." It is clear, nonetheless, that knowledge of self which leads to the knowledge of God does not mean merely the metaphysical self, but also reason, mind, the body of vital principle. This philosophical view was well known to al-Ghazzali. According to Socrates, " 'Know thyself' means that one should tend to his own soul, and then so far as it is possible, to help others in tending theirs." For Confucius the aim of knowing oneself is to make man virtuous, and one can know what it is to be virtuous by studying human relationships.[8]

Al-Ghazali not only accepts these Greek, Islamic, and Chinese ideas of self-knowledge, but he goes further by saying that the purpose of Sufism is to enable man to obtain communion with his *Beloved*, the Supreme Being. This communion holds both ways: man in communion with God and God in communion with man. The ideal man according to al-Ghazzali is the ideal image of God. The elect, or the ideal man is one who is assured by God's interest in him.

From Neoplatonism and Plotinian teaching, al-Ghazzali derived his idea of emanation. In Plotinian teaching the first emanation from the *One* was universal mind. (The term al-Ghazzali uses is *Al-Aql-Al-Awaval*.) When God wishes to bestow revelation on a creature, He makes use of the First Intelligence. Human intelligence is derived from Universal Intelligence as the light from the sun.[9] From the Universal Mind emanates the Universal Soul, which in its turn gives rise to the phenomenal world and to individual human souls. "The human soul," says Plotinus, "is a Divine thing, belonging to another order than that of sense. The human soul resembles the Divine Nature in containing three principles: the intellectual, which is the true self; the reasoning soul, which represents the normal human life; and the animal soul, which is the unreasonable nature of man."[10]

Likewise al-Ghazzali argues that the universal soul is related to universal mind as Eve is to Adam, and that the universal mind is next to it in honor and nobility and receptivity—the second emanation from the One, the One from which all individual souls proceed. He believes that the human soul is divine, belonging not to the sensual, but the spiritual world. "The human soul includes the highest self (*Al Nafs Al-Mutm'inna*) which he also calls the rational soul (*Al Nafs Al-Natiga*), identified with the heart and the spirit of man which is divine in its origin. There is, secondly, the reproachful soul (*Al Nafs Al-Lawama*) which predominates in the normal human being, in which the voice of conscience is at work to correct the downward pull of the flesh. And thirdly, there is the headstrong soul (*Al Nafs Al-Ammara*) which is the irrational self, under the control of the animal nature."[11]

It was from Neoplatonism that al-Ghazzali obtained his idea of God not only as light, but as Supreme Beauty and Supreme Love—as the natural inclination of the soul towards beauty, whether terrestrial or divine. According to al-Ghazzali, "The eye delights in looking upon what is beautiful, and the ear in listening to beautiful music, but goodness and beauty exist in other than objects of sense, in character and knowledge and conduct and the virtues. It cannot be denied that where beauty exists, it is natural to love it. The greater the beauty, the greater the love, and since complete and perfect beauty is found only in God, He alone can be worthy of true love."[12]

He also accepted the theory of the seven Heavens, which played a part in Platonic and Neoplatonic thought. These conceptions and others with traces of a Neoplatonic origin found in his writings were derived from his own personal study of the Greek writers in Arabic translation or from the works of al-Kindi (b.873), considered to be the founder of Muslim philosophy. Furthermore, he studied the works of al-Farabi and accepted his Neoplatonic theory of emanation which emphasized the desire of the human being to enter into the closest union with universal mind. Al-Ghazzali also often drew upon Jewish and Christian sources to illustrate his mystical teachings.

3

Al-Ghazzali enjoys a unique position in the history of Sufism. The eclectic method produced in al-Ghazzali a great thinker and teacher who systematized Sufi doctrines and gave them clarity, precision, and purpose. He rejected formalism, attacked the corruption of the state and church, and introduced the idea that true religion must always be a matter of personal experience. Lamenting the decadence of the faith, he states that "the guides of the path of the future life are the learned who are the successors of the messengers of Allah." However, because of the fact that the prophets lived a long time ago, learned men have become increasingly concerned with formalism. Furthermore, everyone, having become passionately enamored with transitory pleasures, has begun to ignore that which is regarded as good. Thus, man argues that the science of religion has become obliterated and the lights of guidance have become effaced in the regions of the earth. "I decided," al-Ghazzali writes, "to compose this book to effect a revitalization of the sciences of religion, to disclose the well-traced paths of the previous religious leaders, and to give a clear explanation to him who wishes to attain the beneficial sciences of the prophets and sound ancestors."[13]

Al-Ghazzali's influence on Islamic religious philosophy may be said to be fourfold:

1. He led Islam away from scholasticism and stress upon theological dogmas to a new study of the Qoran and Muhammad's simple life and his universal teachings.

2. He stressed the element of hope more than that of fear.

3. It was through his efforts that Sufism attained a respected and an assured position within Islam.

4. He brought philosophy and intellectual thinking within the grasp of the common man.

In the history of Islam and Sufism, al-Ghazzali enjoys the status of a thinker who adopted the doctrines of other Sufi leaders and systematized, criticized, clarified, and elaborated on them. In contradiction to the orthodox religious leaders and philosophers, al-Ghazzali places stress upon personal experience in religious beliefs. He contends that the truth of religion depends not on miracles, laws, or rites and rituals, but on the soul's experience and communion. He states that there are three stages of belief or certainty: first, the simple belief of the multitude who follow the opinions of leaders without questioning their authenticity; secondly, the advanced knowledge of the learned, gained through books; finally, the supreme belief acquired through experience.[14]

T. J. DeBoer recognizes al-Ghazzali as the most remarkable figure in all Islam: "Although he abandoned the attempt to understand this world, he comprehended much more profoundly than did the philosophers the religious problems of his time. These philosophers were intellectual in their methods, like their Greek predecessors, and consequently regarded religious doctrine as merely the product of the conception or fancy or even caprice of the lawgiver."[15]

But al-Ghazzali divided spiritual life into practical experience, which means dedicated action, and the contemplative, which eventually would lead into revelation. The practical religious action which begins with service and love of others leads on to the contemplative stage which brings one to the direct intuitive experience of God. This latter experience is attained only by meditation and inward contemplation which is more gratifying than the vision of our eyes. Through contemplative knowledge, claimed al-Ghazzali, the veil would be raised and the divine glory would be revealed so clearly that it could not be doubted; and this would be possible to man, if the heart, which is the mirror, were not dimmed by impurity. In proportion, as the heart was polished and turned towards truth, the Divine Reality would be manifested. This could be attained only through self-discipline, knowledge, and service.[16]

According to A. J. Arberry, al-Ghazzali "brought out various aspects of the moral, metaphysical, and mystical system in which he essayed to reconcile Sufism with Muslim orthodoxy and to prove that the Muslim life of devotion to the one God could not be lived perfectly save by following the Sufi way."

Al-Ghazzali was convinced that Islam could be saved only through moral perfection and that that could be attained only through "the Sufi path," which was not dependent upon an authority derived from others, nor upon knowledge obtained by study, but which had developed through love and service. Believing that the universe was the manifestation of God, he regarded man as a microcosm that was equally the manifestation of God on a smaller scale. His estimate that man was the image of the Divine indicates that al-Ghazzali took a lofty view of man's spiritual possibilities. It means that man, possessed of will, must himself take an active and strenuous part in seeking to realize his great possibilities. Man is endowed with the reasoning faculty which enables him to understand intelligibles and make de-

ductions therefrom and both mind and will must be
employed in bringing both into conformity with the mind
and the will of God.

4

Al-Ghazzali's influence was great during his lifetime. His
lectures, his books, and his teachings won him both commendation and condemnation. For every critic there were
scores of admirers and followers who studied al-Ghazzali's
works and used them as mystical, philosophical, and
theological authorities. Al-Ghazzali's influence made itself
felt throughout the length and breadth of Islam. His books
are still read and widely and thoroughly studied. "But it was
not only within Islam that his teaching was studied and
accepted and made a rule of life. Those of other faiths, both
in the East and West, found much in his writings to be
admired and much of his teachings on the mystic way which
could be adopted by mystics who owed no allegiance to
Islam."[17] His works were studied with great interest in all
the universities of Europe. Within a century after his death,
translations of his works in Hebrew and Latin appeared in
Spain, Italy, and France, exercising a great influence on
medieval Jewish and Christian thought. Jewish writers
found similarities between al-Ghazzali's mystical writings
and the *Zohar*, a Jewish mystical treatise compiled from
many sources, which appeared in Spain in the thirteenth
century. Al-Ghazzali's book, *The Mishkat Al-Anwar*, was
translated by Isaac Alfase and quoted by the sixteenth-
century writer Moses ibn-Habib, a native of Lisbon, who
was himself a poet, philosopher and teacher. Remond, the
Archbishop of Toledo from A.D. 1130 to 1150, who
founded a college of translators and commentators there
under the Archdeacon Dominic Gondisolvi, encouraged
the translation of the most important Arabic works on philosophy and science to Latin. Amongst these translations

were the works of ibn-Sina, al-Farabi, and al-Ghazzali.

In 1231, Frederick II, Emperor of the Holy Roman Empire, began to reorganize the kingdom of Sicily. Both in Sicily and in the course of his visits to Palestine, Frederick established close contact with Muslims. He learned Arabic and studied the work of the Muslim thinkers in general and the Sufi doctrines in particular. Greatly attracted to them, he adopted Middle Eastern costumes and customs. The views ascribed to Frederick show that his ideas were based on the writings of al-Ghazzali and other Sufi thinkers who regarded all religions as equally tolerable and believed in a universal God who had created man in His own image. In the end Frederick became such a great admirer of the Sufi way of life that some of his enemies in Rome represented him as a free-thinker who regarded all religions and their rituals as worthless. They attributed to him the statement that the world had suffered from three great impostors: Moses, Christ, and Muhammad. Despite the fact that Frederick denied the statement and professed a favorable attitude towards the three great religious leaders, Pope Gregory in his famous encyclical letter, *Ad omnes principes et prelatos terrae,* compared Frederick to the blaspheming beast of Revelation XIII; Frederick, in reply, likened the Pope to the beast described in Revelation VI; thus conflict and controversy continued.

By the end of the thirteenth century Arabic thought had spread significantly into Europe. St. Thomas Aquinas (d. 1274), who studied at the University of Naples, admitted his indebtedness to al-Ghazzali and other Muslim philosophers. Unquestionably he is regarded as a great Christian authority on the works of al-Farabi, ibni-Sina, al-Ghazzali, and ibni-Roshd. He draws freely upon the mysticism and philosophy of the Greeks and Muslims and coordinates them with Christian theology.

In reference to the inability of the creature to realize the majesty of the creator, St. Thomas uses the very words of al-Ghazzali in saying that "the sun, though supremely visible, cannot be seen by the bat, because of its excess light." Again, in dealing with the spiritual aspiration of the human soul, due to its affinity with the bizarre, St. Thomas states that the ultimate perfection of the rational creature is to be found in that which is the principle of its being, since a thing is perfect insofar as it attains to that principle. God is the greatest of all gods and He alone is true perfection. He is the end towards which all things move in order to achieve the perfection which can be given by Him alone, which has become like Him. Man must find out wherein his own perfection consists and then seek to pursue it. He was not created simply for sensual satisfaction, for this is common to both man and the brutes, nor for the pursuit of material ends, for man shares the nature of the angels as well as that of the brutes. This argument is set forth by al-Ghazzali in almost the same terms in his book *Kimiya Al Saadat* and elsewhere.[18]

The real home of the works of al-Ghazzali, ibn-Sina, and ibn-Roshd was at the University of Bologna and at its sister University of Padua. From these two centers the work of Muslim philosophers and Sufi thinkers effectively spread over all Italy, including Venice and Ferrara, until the seventeenth century. Muslim influence was especially predominant at Bologna, because Frederick II had presented the university with copies of the Latin translations prepared by his order from Arabic.[19]

One notable example of Muslim and Sufi influence in Italy is found in Dante Alighieri (1265–1321), who admitted his indebtedness to al-Ghazzali and quoted him in most of his works. "The ascent through the Seven Heavens, where the blessed dwell in accordance with their spiritual merits, described in the *Paradiso*, has been recognized as derived from Muslim legends of the Prophet's ascent to Heaven; al-Ghazzali gives a version of it in which the guardian angels ascend through the Seven Heavens, bearing the good deeds of believers, none of which are acceptable to God unless for His sake alone."[20] Dante, like al-Ghazzali, describes himself as one who, while still in the flesh "had come from time to the eternal." Conceiving of religion as an experience of eternity, he held that the soul, even in this life, can unite itself with the Divine. He believed in the possibility and the actuality of certain experiences by which the mind is brought into contact with what it believes to be God and enjoys fruition of what it takes as the ultimate reality.[21] Dante accepts al-Ghazzali's statement that, while scholasticism is the body of religion, mysticism is the soul, and love the animating spirit of both: "Love, truly taken and subtly considered is nought else than spiritual union of the soul and of the thing loved; to which union the soul, of her own nature, responds swiftly or slowly, according to the degree to which she is free or impeded."[22]

Dante's statement that goodness arouses love, and the greater the goodness and perfection, the greater the love, is a quotation from *Alihya*, al-Ghazzali's master work. It contains the conception that God is the light supernal, "from whom light is radiated to all other things, which kindles the lights celestial and the lights terrestrial, which are lit by that light as the lamp is lit by fire for He is essential light, elemental fire. The vision, for those who attain, is the contemplation of that light and those who look upon it pass away into it."[23] Like St. Thomas, Dante adopted this Sufi conception of the Beatific Vision and elaborated upon it in his works. To Dante vision is light; the divine essence is conceived of as a living light going forth in creation, kindling the lower lights from its own radiance, a divine sun "which kindles all and each."[24]

5

In an age of prejudice, bigotry, and religious intolerance, al-Ghazzali advocated and practiced tolerance. He often advised Muslims to take pious Christians, Jews, and Hindus as their models of religious practice. In fact, in all his works the universal nature of man and intellectual truth and decency are emphasized. His doctrine of emanation was derived from Neoplatonic writings. His criticism of causality predated David Hume's parallel theories by several centuries, and he exerted great influence over William of Ockham and other Christian philosophers.

Al-Ghazzali's statement that the concept of causality cannot be gained from material given by the senses was adopted by Ockham. To connect one occurrence with another by the notion of cause and effect is the result not of rational knowledge but of a habit of expecting perception of a second occurrence after having perceived the first, because that sequence has previously taken place in innumerable cases. Al-Ghazzali believed that causality worked, but that reason was not capable of understanding: The propensity to believe in the existence of the world and in man's faculty to think and judge was stronger than the awareness of the limits of human reason.

Al-Ghazzali's influence on William of Ockham was so profound that the latter rejected many prevalent assumptions of the Medieval Church. Ockham, like al-Ghazzali, decided to teach men to think, and the result of his teachings was the elaboration of mystic ideas, the reduction of the influence of the Church in human society, and the preparation for a new interpretation of the physical world. He followed al-Ghazzali in rejecting all attempts to evade reason. He denounced all those who claimed to know the psychology of God, and he flatly denied the usefulness and truth of the speculations of all the great Doctors of the

Church. He also held ethics to be independent of metaphysics.

Al-Ghazzali's description of the nature of man is enlightening:

> Though man shares with the other animals external and internal senses, he is at the same time also endowed with two qualities peculiar to himself, knowledge and will. By knowledge is meant the power of generalization, the conception of abstract ideas, and the possession of intellectual truths. By will is meant that strong desire to acquire an object which after due consideration of its consequences has been pronounced by reason to be good. It is quite different from animal desire; indeed, it is often the very opposite of it.

> In the beginning children also lack these two qualities. They have passion, anger, and all the external and internal senses, but will find its expression only later. Knowledge differs according to the truth and contemplation of God, is contented with bodily devotions and acquirement of means of living. Such a mind, though pure, will not reflect the divine image, for his objects of thought are other than this. If this is the condition of such a mind, think what will be the state of those minds which are absorbed in the gratification of their inordinate passions.

> An external screen may, as it were, come before the objects. Sometimes a man who has subjugated his passions still, through blind imitation or prejudice, fails to know the truth. Such types are found amongst the votaries of the Kalam. Even many virtuous men also fall prey to it and blindly stick to their dogmas.

> There may be ignorance of the means for the acquisition of truth. Thus for illustration, a man wants to see his back in a mirror: if he places the mirror before his eyes he fails to see his back; if he keeps it facing his back it will still be out of sight. Let him then take another mirror and place one before his eyes and the other facing his back in such a position that the image of the latter is reflected in

the former. Thus he will be able to see his back. Similarly
the knowledge of the unknown from the known.

The divine dispensation is liberal in the distribution of its
bounties, but for reasons mentioned above, minds fail to
profit by them. For human minds partake of the nature of
the divine, and the capacity to apprehend truth is innate.
The Qoran says: "Surely we offered the trust to the heavens
and the earth and the mountains, but they declined to bear
it up and were afraid of it and man took it up. Surely he is
not just (to himself) and is ignorant." In this passage the
innate capacity of man is hinted at and refers to the secret
power of knowing God, latent in human minds by virtue of
which they have preference over other objects and the universe. The Prophet says: "Every child is born in the right
state (*Fitrat*) but his parents make him a Jew, a Christian, or
a Magician," and again: "Had it not been that evil spirits
hover round the hearts of the sons of Adam they would
have seen the kingdom of heaven." Ibn-Umar reports that
the Prophet was once asked where God is found, whether
on earth or in heaven. "He is in the hearts of his faithful
servants," replied the Prophet. It will not be out of place to
throw some light here on the following terms which are
often vaguely applied while dealing with the question of
human nature:

1. *Qalb* (heart) has two meanings. (a) A cone-shaped
piece of flesh on the left side of the chest, circulating blood,
the source of animal spirits. It is found in all animals. The
heart thus belongs to the external world and can be seen
with the material eyes. (b) A mysterious divine substance
which is related to the material heart, like the relation between the dweller and the house, or the artisan and his
implements. It alone is sentient and responsible.

2. *Ruh* (spirit) means (a) A vapory substance which issues

from the material heart and quickens every part of the body. It is like a lamp which is placed in a house and sheds its light on all sides. (b) The soul, which is expressed in the Qoran as "divine commandment" and is used in the same sense as the second meaning of *Qalb*, mentioned above.

3. *Nafs* (self) which means (a) The substratum for appetite and passion. The Sufis call it the embodiment of vices. (b) The ego which receives different names in accordance with the qualities acquired from changes in its conditions. When in subjugating passions it acquires mastery over them and feels undisturbed, it is called *the peaceful self* (*Nafsi lauwama*). When it freely indulges in the gratification of its passions, it is called *the inordinate self* (*Nafsi ammara*).[25]

6

Al-Ghazzali ranks equally with Rumi and Shabastari in his emphasis on the Sufi doctrine that life without true love is a farce, that love is the guiding star of the mystic way, and that true love eventually leads one to the ultimate truth. A summary of the contributions of al-Ghazzali will reinforce his place in history and in spiritual theology:

1. He introduced speculation and innovation into orthodox Islam.

2. He argued for freedom of the will: God creates power in the man and also creates choice; man then creates the act corresponding to this power and choice.

3. Unlike ibn-Roshd, al-Ghazzali emphasized suprarational intuition attained in a state of ecstasy as the proper means whereby the soul is raised above the world of shadow and reflection to the light of reality.

4. He popularized the use of philosophy by arguing that it is no more than common sense, and he regulated the thinking which should be employed by men in considering religion or any other subject.

5. He rendered philosophy and theology subordinate to personal experience and revelation in man's relation to the ultimate truth: "To reach the plane of reality man must be raised by spiritual faculty, by which he perceives the invisible things."

6. He liberated Sufism from the rigid formalism and conservatism of the Islamic church.[26]

7. He paved the way for the development of the pantheistic system of philosophy followed by ibn-al-Arabi, Jalal Uddin Rumi, and Shabastari.

8. He introduced many Christian ideas and teachings into Sufism. There are many quotations in his books taken directly from the New Testament. He finds great inspiration in Christ's life and teachings and uses them for the development of his mystical doctrine:

"Blessed are the meek upon this earth for they shall be honored on the Day of Judgment." "Blessed are the peacemakers in this life, for they shall inherit Heaven in their next life." "Blessed are the pure in heart for they will see the face of God on the day of Resurrection."

His book, *Al-Ihyaul Ulumad-Din*, contains many quotations from St. Paul. Referring to the Beatific vision, al-Ghazzali quotes the Apostle: God has prepared for His faithful servants "what eye hath not seen, nor ear heard, and what has not entered into the heart of man."[27]

One also finds a great resemblance between al-Ghazzali's spiritual and mystical experience and that of St. Augustine: "Beautiful forms are love for their own sake; the very perception of beauty is a cause of delight, and it is undeniable that it is loved for its own sake. So all green things and running water are loved. It is natural to delight in the sight of the celestial lights."

1. G. M. Wickens, *The Legacy of Persia* (edited by Arberry), p. 170.
2. *Ibid.*

3. Al-Ghazzali, *Mizan al-Amal*, quoted by Margaret Smith, *Al-Ghazzali the Mystic*, Luzac and Company Ltd., London, 1944, p. 11.
4. *Ibid.*
5. According to al-Murtada Az Zabidi (d. 1205), "The final straw which caused Abu-Hamid al-Ghazzali to break the bonds with this world came one day when his brother Ahmad entered while he was preaching and recited:
    You lent a hand to them when they hung back, and you yourself have been kept behind, whilst they went ahead of you.
    You have taken the role of guide, yet you will not be guided; you preach but do not listen.
    O whetstone, how long will you whet iron, but will not let yourself be whetted?"
6. Al-Ghazzali, *Almungidh Min Adh dhalal*, trans. by Montgomery Watt, George Allen and Unwin, London, 1953, p. 30.
7. *Ibid.*, pp. 54, 55.
8. DeBoer, T. J.; *The History of Philosophy in Islam*, Luzac and Company Ltd., London, 1963, pp. 162–67.
9. *Katab Al-Maarif, Al Aqliyya*, quoted by Margaret Smith, *Al-Ghazzali*, p. 106.
10. Plotinus, *Ennead*, III, V. I., pp. 6–10.
11. *Al-Risalat al Laduniyya*, quoted by Margaret Smith in *Al-Ghazzali*, pp. 106–109.
12. Al-Ghazzali, *Alihya*, Book IV, p. 257.
13. *Alihya al Ulumuddin* (The Resurrection of the Science of Religion), vol. 1, pp. 2–3.
14. Al-Ghazzali, *Book of Fear and Hope*, translated by William McKane, E. J. Brill, Leiden, pp. x–xix.
15. DeBoer, *op. cit.*, p. 168.
16. Al-Ghazzali, *Alihya, op. cit.*, pp. 4–48.
17. Margaret Smith, *Al-Ghazzali, the Mystic, op. cit.*, p. 62.
18. *Summa Theologiae*, Part 1, Q. XII, Q. I and Q. II, Quoted by Margaret Smith, *Al-Ghazzali*, pp. 220–21.
19. DeLacy O'Leary, *Arabic Thought and Its Place in History*, London, Routledge & Kegan Paul Ltd; 1954, pp. 288–91.
20. Margaret Smith, *Al-Ghazzali, op. cit.*, p. 224.
21. Edmund Gardener, *Dante and the Mystics*, Octagon Books, Inc., New York, 1955, pp. 1–13.
22. *Ibid.*
23. Al-Ghazzali, *Mishkatal-Anvar*, pp. 110, 117, 144, translated by Margaret Smith.
24. Dante, *Paradiso* XIII, p. 52; XXIII, pp. 28–30.
25. Dagobert D. Runes (editor), *Treasury of Philosophy;* Philosophical Library, New York, 1955, pp. 33–38.
26. O'Leary, *op. cit.*, pp. 209–24.
27. Epistle to the Corinthians II, 9.

5

Jalal Ud-Din Rumi, Light of Sufism

Do not wish ill to anyone, O man of good nature,
Whether they be people of the church or the synagogue,
What a bad place is a bad thought: Hell springs from it.
Know that the Joys of Paradise are from good thoughts alone.

Sufi motto

A characteristic of Sufism is its use of the earthly language of love and passion to express ecstatic communion with the Divine. The following discussion of some of the most celebrated of the Persian poets who represent the loftiest expression of love and beauty is limited only by the space allotted to this discourse.

The great poets of Persia who have spoken the Sufi language fall into two classes. The first group, by using the words "lovers," "beloved," "wine," "beauty," and "women" with cleverness and ambiguity, "entrance the sinner and evoke sublime raptures in the saint. For these free-thinkers, orthodox Islam, no matter how the ordinary citizen might lean upon it, was a broken reed. Scorning the barren virtue of orthodoxy and cloister, admitting no guidance but Divine illumination, they pressed their points to the brink of libertinism."[1]

A second group of poets based their poetry on a lofty ethical and moral system, which represents purity of heart, service to God and man, love, ecstasy, dedication to the truth, union, self-renunciation and control of the passions; all necessary conditions of external happiness. Although on the surface these poets did not openly assail orthodox Islam, they delivered many indirect attacks. Frequently one detects in their writings the idea that all religions and divine revelations are only the rays of a single eternal sun; that all prophets have delivered—only in different languages— the same principles of goodness, truth, and love which flow from the divine soul of the world.[2] The leader of this school of thought is Jalal-Ud-din Rumi (1207–1273), who believed ethics to be subservient to philosophy. Virtue, according to Rumi, is not an end but a means: The end is union with God through love:

O Thou who art my soul's comfort in the season of sorrow,
O Thou who art my spirit's treasure in the bitterness of
    death!
That which the imagination hath not conceived, that which
    the understanding hath not seen,
Visiteth my soul from Thee; hence in worship I turn to-
    ward Thee.
By Thy Grace I keep fixed on eternity my amorous gaze,
Except, O King, the pomps that perish lead me astray.
The favour of him who brings glad tidings of Thee,
Even without Thy summons, is sweeter in mine ear than
    songs.
If the never-ceasing Bounty should offer kingdoms,
If the Hidden Treasure should set before me all that is,
I would bow down with my soul, I would lay my face in the
    dust,
I would cry, 'Of all these the love of such an One for me!'

The mystic ascends to the Throne in a moment; the ascetic
   needs a month for one day's journey.
Although, for the ascetic, one day is of great value, yet how
   should his one day be equal to fifty thousand years?
In the life of the adept, every day is fifty thousand of the
   years of this world.
Love *(mahabbat)*, and ardent love *('ishq)* also, is an attribute
   of God; Fear is an attribute of the slave to lust and appetite.

Love hath five hundred wings, and every wing reaches
   from above the empyrean to beneath the earth.
The timorous ascetic runs on foot; the lovers of God fly
   more quickly than lightning.
May Divine favour free thee from this wayfaring! None but
   the royal falcon hath found the way to the King.[3]

2

In Rumi, the Persian mystical genius found its supreme
expression. In the vast landscape of Sufi poetry, he stands
out as a reverend mentor. His example has influenced all
the succeeding generations, and every literate Persian has
read and paid homage to the work of the respected "prince
of faith." For Rumi, "the world is nonexistent," states
Reynold A. Nicholson, "and he will not study the unreal;
like the compass he circles ever round a point, on which his
thoughts, action and very being depend: he cannot stray
from his course any more than a star can leave its orbit." All
mystical experiences are the record of one spiritual experience and are pervaded by a single overpowering emotion.
The language of all mystics is the same. "How often do
Emerson and Shelley remind us of Rumi. Juan de La Cruz
has indited lyrics which would be easy to mistake for translations from the Rumi *Divan*."[4]

Sufi theosophy, the source of Rumi's inspiration, had
been fashioned before him by two great Sufi teachers, Sanai

of Ghazna and Attar of Nishapur. From these sources, *Masnawi* and *Divan* descend by different channels. "The one is a majestic river, calm and deep, meandering through many a rich and varied landscape to the immeasurable ocean; the other a foaming torrent that leaps and plunges in the ethereal solitude of the hills."[5] The *Masnawi* is commonly called in Iran the "Persian Qoran." Rumi predicted in one of his verses: "My *Masnawi*, like the glorious Qoran, will be praised by many and resented and condemned by few."

The following lines from this work explain some of Rumi's ideas of man and his relationship with his creator:

> The man of God is drunk without wine.
> The man of God is full without meat.
> The man of God is distraught and bewildered.
> The man of God has no food or sleep.
> The man of God is a treasure in a ruin.
> The man of God is not of air and earth.
> The man of God is not of fire and water.
> The man of God is a boundless sea.
> The man of God rains pearls without a cloud.
> The man of God hath a hundred moons and skies,
> The man of God hath a hundred suns.
> The man of God is made wise by the Truth,
> The man of God is not learned from the books.
> The man of God is beyond infidelity and religion,
> To the man of God right and wrong are alike.

Rumi once met a sage by the name of Shamsi Tabriz. The man was despotic and overbearing, but his tremendous spiritual enthusiasm, based on the conviction that he was a chosen spokesman of God, enchanted Rumi. Sultan Walad, Rumi's son, describes the passionate and uncontrollable emotion which overwhelmed Rumi during the days of his association with Shamsi Tabriz in the following words:

Never for a moment did he cease from listening to music
  and dancing,
Never did he rest by day or night.
He had been a *mufti* (religious leader); he became a poet;
He had been an ascetic; he became intoxicated by love.
'Twas not the wine of the grape: The illumined soul drinks
  only the wine of light.[6]

"Jalal-ud-din's acquaintance with this mysterious person-
age began at Qonya in December, 1244, lasted with ever-
increasing intimacy for fifteen months, and was brought to
an abrupt close in March, 1246, by the violent death of
Shamsi Tabriz." The strong passions, the sudden death of
Shams, and the devotion of Rumi to him are reminiscent of
the story of Socrates and Plato. Rumi dedicated one of his
works to the sage—*Divan Shamsi Tabriz.*

I have no business save carouse and revelry.
If once in my life I spent a moment without thee,
From that time and from that hour I regret my life.
If once in this world I win a moment with thee,
I will trample on both worlds, I will dance in triumph
  forever,
O Shamsi Tabriz, I am so drunken in this world,
That except of drunkenness and revelry I have no tale to
  tell.

When Rumi was asked to describe a Sufi, he answered:
"What makes the Sufi? Purity of heart; not the patched
mantle and the lust perverse of those vile earth-bound men
who steal his name."

> He in all dregs discerns the essence pure.
> In hardship ease, in tribulation joy.
> The phantom sentries, who with batons drawn
> Guard beauty's palace gate and curtains lower,
> Give way before him, unafraid he passes,
> And showing the King's arrow, enters in.[7]

The enraptured man, according to Rumi, has passed beyond the illusion of subject and object, broken through to
the oneness and feels the cosmic consciousness:

If there be any lover in the world, O Muslims, 'tis I,
If there be any believer, infidel, or Christian hermit, 'tis I,
The wine-dregs, the cupbearers, the minstrel, the harp, and
   the music
The beloved, the candle, the drink and the joy of the
   drunken, 'tis I.
The two and seventy creeds and sects in the world do not
   really exist:
I swear by God that every creed and sect 'tis I.[8]

> Ere the world wastes,
> Sleep no more: arise.
> The caravan hastes,
> The sweet scent dies.
>
> Remembering thy lip,
> The ruby red I kiss;
> Having not that to sip,
> My lips press this
> Not to thy far sky
> Reaches my stretched hand,
> Wherefore, kneeling, I
> Embrace thy hand.[9]

Rumi states that music awakens in the soul a memory of
celestial harmonies heard in a state of pre-existence, before
the soul was separated from God:

> 'Tis said, the pipe and flute that charm our ears
> Derive their melody from rolling spheres;
> But faith, o'erpassing speculations' bound,
> Can see what sweetness every jangled sound.
> We, who are poets of Adam, heard with him
> The song of angels and of seraphim.
> Our memory, though dull and sad, retains

Some echo still of those unearthly strains.
Oh, music is the meat of all who love,
Music uplifts the soul to realms above.
The shades glow, the latent fires increase:
We listen and are fed with joy and peace.[10]

In the following verses, Rumi describes the doctrine of
the flute and destiny:

We are the flute, our music is all Thine:
We are the mountains echoing only Thee;
Pieces of chess Thou marshallest in life
And movest to defeat or victory;
Lions emblazoned high on flags unfurled
Thy wind invisible sweeps us through the world.[11]

Rumi's best-known poem is the "Song of the Flute," sung
by all the Sufis. Unfortunately, none of its beauty, charm,
emotional qualities, delicacy and mystical idioms can be
adequately reproduced in translation. Much of the beauty
of his poetry is lost or falls flat:

Hear, how yon flute in sadly pleasing tales
Departed bliss and present woe bewails.
With me, from native banks untimely torn,
Love-warbling youths and soft-eyed virgins mourn.

O let the heart, by fatal absence rent,
Feel what I sing, and bleed when I lament:
Who roams in exile from his parent bough
Pants to return, and chides each ang'ring hour.
My notes, in circles of the grave and gay,
Have hail'd the rising, cheered the closing day:
Each in my fond affections claim'd a part,
Oh, more than Galen learn'd, than Plato wise.
My guide, my law, my joy supreme arise.
Love warms this frigid clay with mystic fire,
And dancing mountains leap with young desire.

Blest is the soul, that swims in seas of love,
And long the life sustain'd by food above.
With forms imperfect can perfection dwell?
Here pause my song, and thou, vain world farewell.[12]

Rumi shows a great respect for all the prophets and their
ideas, but he is suspicious of organized religion, firmly believing that the ordinary theologian is in the bondage of his
vested interest and enslaved to dogmas and creeds. God is
everywhere except in the shrines which are established by
religious institutions:

Cross and the churches, from end to end
I surveyed; He was not on the cross.
I went to the idol temple, to the ancient pagoda,
No trace was visible there.
I bent the reins of search to the Ka'ba,
He was not in that resort of old and young.

I gazed into my own heart;
There I saw Him, He was nowhere else.
In the whirl of its transport my spirit was tossed,
Till each atom of separate being I lost.

When "I" and "Thou" become one
There is no need for mosque, synagogue or church.

The prophet said, that God hath declared,
I am not contained in aught above or below,
I am not contained in earth, or sky, or even
In highest heaven, know this for a surety, O beloved:
I am contained in the believer's heart.
If you seek me, search in such hearts.[13]

Jalal-ud-din had very little patience with the Muslim
clergy. He believed that they were superficial, petty, and
narrow-minded. He asks scornfully:

Do you know a name without a thing answering to it?
Have you ever plucked a rose from R, O, S, E?
You name His name, go, seek the reality named by it.
Look for the moon in the sky, not in the water.
If you desire to rise above mere names and letters,
Make yourself free from self at one stroke.
Become pure from all attributes of self.
That you may see your own bright essence,
Yea, see in your own heart the knowledge of the prophet,
Without book, without tutor, without preceptor.[14]

Rumi's discovery of self is one of the great fascinating
achievements of his work. He argues that man's understanding of self is the climax or the last stage of the progress
of the soul. At this stage the soul rises beyond reason and
knowledge "to a state of unconscious rapture, where seer
and seen are no more distinct, seeker is one with sought,
lover with beloved." At this stage our selves are inseparable
from the world and its creator. We become cognizant of a
world in which our human drama is being carried on by us.
To Rumi, the self is not determined by class, creed, or color.
It is conditioned by virtues based on love and service.

I have put duality away, I have seen that the words are one;
One I seek, One I know, One I see, One I call.
He is the first, He is the last, He is outward, He is the
    inward. . . .[15]

To Rumi, discovery of self involves the perception that
universal mind and universal soul exist, and we have to
nurture them through motivation and personal experience
in order to achieve absolute unity with God. It is how man's
experience elicits personal responses that matters. The
forces outside provoke but do not form man's reply. We
cannot withdraw from others or from the world. We have
to integrate our souls and our sense of others into the uni-

versal soul and into a universal mind which is the home of ideas and the true archetype of the phenomenal world. This freedom to improve the self is infinite:

From the pure star-bright souls replenishment is ever coming to the stars of heaven.
Outwardly we are ruled by these stars, but our inward nature has become the ruler of the skies.
Therefore, while in form thou art the microcosm, in reality thou art the macrocosm.
Externally the branch is the origin of the fruit, intrinsically the branch came into existence for the sake of the fruit.
Had there been no hope of the fruit, would the gardener have planted the tree?
Therefore in reality the tree is born of the fruit, though it appears to be produced by the tree.

Muhammad Iqbal (1877–1938), the great poet and mystic philosopher of Pakistan, in his first Persian poem quoted the famous couplet which opens Rumi's *Masnawi*:

Hear, how yon flute in sadly pleasing tales
Departed bliss and present woe bewails.

Iqbal was an advocate of the spiritual development of love between man and a personal God and of the infinite quest for goodness. He regarded the Qoran and Rumi's *Masnawi* as the two basic and most expedient books for man's spiritual formtion. Iqbal calls Rumi "the lamp of the way of the free man." "The Song of the Flute" made such a great impression on Iqbal that he stated:

The beauty of love gets from his reed
A lot of the majesty of divine grandeur.

Rumi's humanitarianism becomes the antithesis of the forces of formalism, rigidity and cold theology. Rumi's poetry—insofar as love is embodied in it—can lead more easily to the living truth than the reasoning of the philosophers and the arguments of theologians. Love flies into the Divine Presence, whereas philosophy and theology lag slowly on the dusty roads. Philosophy and theology endeavor to find the origin of the world and of life, but love is concerned with man's spiritual growth and harmony at the present time. It would be the ideal solution to all the problems of this disturbed and chaotic world if reason and heart, meditation and analytical research, which are fundamentally offsprings of the same divine root, could work together and if men set aside their religious, racial and color prejudices and hatred:

Lo, for I to myself am unknown, now in God's Name what must I do?
I adore not the cross nor the crescent, I am not a Christian nor a Jew.
East nor West, land nor sea is my home, I have kin not with angel nor gnome,
I am wrought not of fire nor of foam, I am shaped not of dust nor of dew.
Not in this world nor that world I dwell, not in Paradise neither in Hell;
Not from Eden and Paradise I fell, not from Adam my lineage I drew.
In a place beyond uttermost place, in a tract without shadow or trace,
Soul and body transcending I live in the soul of my loved one anew.[16]

There was, in Iqbal's opinion, only one poet in the West who might be compared to Rumi, and that was Goethe: Both of them greater than poets, both "not prophets but possessing a book," both of them teaching immortal yearning and the quest for the loftiest levels of the Divine life, both advocating spiritual growth and both attributing the greatest importance, not to cold materialism, but to love. "Alas," Iqbal laments, "there will rise no other Rumi from the rose-garden of Iran. I follow Rumi's religion of love":

From the intoxicated eye of Rumi I borrowed
Joy from the rank of divine grandeur.
I have learned the subtleties from *Pir Rumi*
I have burnt myself in his letters.
It is time that I reopen the tavern of Rumi;
The Shaikhs of the Ka'ba are lying drunk in the courtyard
   of the church.[17]

R. A. Nicholson writes:

In Rumi the Persian mystical genius found its supreme expression. Viewing the vast landscape of Sufi poetry we see him standing out as a sublime mountain-peak; the many other poets before and after him are but foot-hills in comparison. The influence of his example, his thought and his language would be powerfully felt through all the succeeding centuries; every Sufi after him capable of reading Persian has acknowledged his unchallenged leadership.[18]

3

Rumi, like al-Ghazzali, was very well acquainted with the ideas of Plotinus and with Neoplatonism. Furthermore, he had met Faridu Din Attar, the great Sufi mentor, on his way to Balkh. He was familiar with the poems of Sanai to whom he pays tribute in one of his odes. One of his biographers mentions his meeting with Sadi who, nevertheless, had very little influence on him. Sadi's odes "are extremely elegant and exceedingly beautiful, but the thoughts will prove to be mostly profane and the diction full of amatory conceits: No revelation of the truth or explanation of the profound mystic path will be found there."[19]

With Attar and Sanai, on the contrary, he was in full

accord. We may conjecture that the first mystical impulse in
Rumi's mind arose from the perusal of the work of these
two poets. They were his mentors and the fountainhead of
his inspiration. He always followed their advice, and accepted them as the soul and eyes of Sufism.

"For the most part Rumi and his mentors are poets inspired in diverse states of reason and love and ecstasy and
intoxication and effacement and mystic dance. Consequently they will not be to all classes dear nor acceptable
to every ear."[20] Rumi sometimes sacrifices literal beauty for
spiritual meanings. His word will always be subject to the
profoundest interpretation. He lacks the color, gaiety, and
subtle humor of Hafiz and does not share Sadi's practical
morality and worldly sagacity. But in greatness of ideas and
loftiness of mystic thoughts he has no peer. "The clearness
of his vision gives a wonderful exaltation to his verse, which
beats against the sky; his odes throb with passion and
rapture-enkindling power."[21]

Up, o ye lovers, and away! 'Tis time to leave the world for
   aye.
Hark, loud and clear from heaven the drum of parting
   calls—let none delay!
The cameleer hath risen amain, made ready all the camel-
   train,
And quittance now desires to gain: why sleep ye, travellers,
   I pray?
Behind us and before there swells the din of parting and of
   bells,
To shoreless space each moment sails a disembodied spirit
   away.
From yonder starry lights, and through those curtain-
   awnings darkly blue.
Mysterious figures float in view, all strange and secret things
   display.
From this orb, wheeling round its pole, a wondrous slumber
   o'er thee stay:

O weary life that weighest naught, o sleep that on my soul
  dost weigh.
O heart, toward thy heart's love wend, and o friend, fly
  toward the friend.
Be wakeful, watchman, to the end: drowse seemingly no
  watchman may.

. . . . .

Happy the moment when we are seated in the palace, thou
  and I,
With two forms and with two figures but with one soul, thou
  and I.
The colours of the grove and the voices of the birds will
  bestow immortality
At the time when we shall come into the garden, thou and I.
The stars of Heaven will come to gaze upon us:
We shall show them the moon herself, thou and I.

. . . . .

Thou and I, individuals no more, shall be mingled in
  ecstasy,
Joyful and secure from foolish babble, thou and I.
All the bright-plumed birds of Heaven will devour their
  hearts with envy
In the place where we shall laugh in such a fashion, thou
  and I.
This is the greatest wonder, that thou and I, sitting here in
  the same nook,
Are at this moment both in Iraq and Khorasan, thou and I.

. . . . .

If you rule your wife outwardly, yet inwardly you are ruled
  by her whom you desire,
This is characteristic of Man: in other animals love is lacking
  and that shows their inferiority.
The Prophet said that woman prevails over the wise, while
  ignorant men prevail over her; for in them the fierceness
  of the animal is immanent.
Love and tenderness are human qualities, anger and lust
  are animal qualities.
Woman is a ray of God: she is not the earthly beloved. She is
  creative: you might say she is not created.

. . . . .

The gnostic is the soul of religion and piety; gnosis is the result of past asceticism.

Asceticism is the labour of sowing; gnosis is the growth and harvesting of the seed.

The gnostic is both the command to do right and the right itself; both the revealer of mysteries and that which is revealed.

He is our King to-day and to-morrow: the husk is for ever a slave to his goodly kernel.

The Faithful are many, but their Faith is one; their bodies are numerous, but their soul is one.

Besides the understanding and soul which is in the ox and the ass, Man has another intelligence and soul.

Again, in the owner of the Divine breath, there is a soul other than the human soul.

The animal soul does not possess oneness: do not seek oneness from that airy spirit.

If its owner eat bread, his neighbour is not filled; if he bear a load, his neighbour does not become laden;

Nay, but he rejoices at his neighbour's death and dies of envy when he sees his neighbour prosperous.

The souls of wolves and dogs are separate; the souls of the Lions of God are united.

I speak nominally of their souls in the plural, for that single Soul is a hundred in relation to the body,

Just as the single light of the sun in heaven is a hundred in relation to the house-courts on which it shines;

But when you remove the walls, all these scattered lights are one and the same.

When the bodily houses have no foundation remaining, the Faithful remain one soul.[22]

All Rumi's stories and messages end with some moral advice or admonition. They are addressed neither to the Persian Sufis nor to the Muslims, but to the whole world:

The unbeliever and the believer both proclaim the praise of God. For God Most High has stated that every man who goes on the right road and practices righteousness, following the sacred law and the way of the prophets and the saints, shall be vouchsafed such happiness and illumination and life. Since both believer and unbeliever practice accordingly, and that which God Most High has promised comes to pass precisely, neither more nor less, it follows then that both proclaim the praises of God, the one with one tongue and the other with another.

So all things, though appearing opposite in relation to their opposites, in relation to the wise man all are performing the same work and are not opposed. Show me the evil thing in this world wherein no good is contained and the good thing wherein no evil is contained.[23]

. . . . .

Thee I choose, of all the world, alone;
Wilt thou suffer me to sit in grief?
My heart is as a pen in thy hand,
Thou art the cause if I am glad or melancholy.
Save what thou willest, what will have I?
Save what thou showest, what do I see?
Thou mak'st grow out of me now a thorn and now a rose;
Now I smell roses and now pull thorns.
If thou keep'st me that, that I am;
If thou wouldst have me this, I am this.
In the vessel where thou givest colour to the soul
Who am I, what is my love and hate?

What is to be done, O Moslems? for I do not recognise
   myself.
I am neither Christian, nor Jew, nor Gabr, nor Moslem.
I am not of the East, nor of the West, nor of the land, nor of
   the sea;
I am not of Nature's mint, nor of the circling heavens.
I am not of earth, nor of water, nor of air, nor of fire;
I am not of the empyrean, nor of the dust, nor of existence,
   nor of entity.
I am not of India, nor of China, nor of Bulgaria, nor of
   Saqsin;

I am not of the Kingdom of 'Iraqain, nor of the country of
   Khorasan.
I am not of this world, nor of the next, nor of Paradise, nor
   of Hell;
I am not of Adam, nor of Eve, nor of Eden and Rizwan.
My place is the Placeless, my trace is the Traceless;
'Tis neither body nor soul, for I belong to the soul of the
   Beloved.

Come, come, for you will not find another friend like me.
Where indeed is a Beloved like me in all the world?
Come, come, and do not spend your life in wandering to
   and fro,
Since there is no market elsewhere for your money.
You are as a dry valley and I as the rain,
You are as a ruined city and I as the architect.
Except my service, which is joy's sunrise,
Man never has felt and never will feel an impression of joy.
You behold in dreams a thousand moving shapes;
When the dream is past you do not see a single one of the
   kind.
Close the eye that sees falsely and open the intellectual eye,
For the senses resemble an ass, and evil desire is the halter.
O thou Who art my soul's comfort in the season of sorrow,
O Thou Who art my spirit's treasure in the bitterness of
   Death!
That which the imagination hath not conceived, that which
   the understanding hath not seen.
Visiteth my soul from Thee; hence in worship I turn to-
   ward Thee.
By Thy Grace I keep fixed on eternity my amorous gaze,
Except, O King, the pomps that perish lead me astray.
The favour of him who brings glad tidings of Thee,
Even without Thy summons, is sweeter in mine ear than
   songs.
If the never-ceasing bounty should offer kingdoms,
If the Hidden Treasure should set before me all that is,
I would bow down with my soul, I would lay my face in the
   dust,
I would cry, "Of all these the love of such an One for Me!

'Twas a fair orchard, full of trees and fruit
And vines and greenery. A Sufi there
Sat with eyes closed, his head upon his knee,
Sunk deep in meditation mystical.
"Why," asked another, "dost thou not behold
These signs of God the Merciful displayed
Around thee, which He bids us contemplate?"
"The signs," he answered, "I behold within;
Without is naught but symbols of the signs."

What is all beauty in the world? The image,
like quivering boughs reflected in a stream,
Of that eternal Orchard which abides
Unwithered in the hearts of Perfect Men.[24]

1. R. A. Nicholson, *Divan Shamsi Tabriz*, Cambridge University Press, 1898 p.p. 25–29.
2. *Ibid.*, p. 26.
3. R. A. Nicholson: *Rumi, Poet and Mystic*, George Allen and Unwin, Ltd., London, 1964. pp. 46 and 102.
4. Rumi, op. cit., p. 25.
5. Rumi's literary work is as stupendous in magnitude as it is sublime in content. It consists of a collection of mystic poems, perhaps as many as twenty-five hundred, which make up the *Divan;* and the *Masnawi*, six books of about twenty-five hundred rhyming couplets.
6. R. A. Nicholson, *Rumi, Poet and Mystic*, George Allen and Unwin Ltd., London, 1964, p. 20.
7. *Ibid.* p. 54
8. Rumi, *Masnawi*, p. 161
9. A. J. Arberry (ed.), *Persian Poems*, pp. 34–39.
10. Rumi, *Masnawi*.
11. Arberry, *op. cit.* p. IX.
12. Translated by Sir William Jones. (A few minor changes made by the authors.)
13. Rumi, translated by E. Sell, *Essays on Islam*, p. 21.
14. *The Mystics of Islam* translated by R. A. Nicholson, pp. 69–70.
15. Rumi, *Divan Shamsi Tabriz*, translated by R. A. Nicholson.
16. *Ibid.*
17. Iqbal, *Divan*, p. 65, Karachi, Pakistan, 1928.
18. Rumi, op. cit., pp. 25–26.
19. *Ibid.*
20. Hedayat, *Majmaul Fasaha*, Teheran, p. 210, 1910
21. J. A. Symonds, *Essays*, vol. II, p. 120, quoted by Nicholson.
22. R. A. Nicholson, *Rumi, Poet and Mystic, op. cit.*
23. Rumi, *Discourses*, transl. A. J. Arberry, *More Tales from the Masnawi*, George Allen and Unwin Ltd., London, 1963, p. 13.
24. R. A. Nicholson, *Rumi, Poet and Mystic, op. cit.* pp. 46–51.

6

Sadi of Shiraz, the Wisdom of Sufism

All Adam's sons are limbs of one another,
Each of the self-same substance as his brothers,
So, while one member suffers ache and grief,
The other members cannot win relief.
Thou, who are heedless of thy brother's pain,
It is not right at all to name thee man.

Sadi

In the Eastern world Sadi of Shiraz enjoys a popularity attained by few writers in the West. "The schoolboy lisps out his first lesson in Sadi's *Gulistan*; the man of learning quotes it; and a vast number of Sadi's expressions have become proverbial. When we consider the time at which it was written—the first half of the thirteenth century—a time when gross darkness brooded over Europe, "the justness of many of his sentiments, and the glorious views of the Divine attributes, contained in his work are truly remarkable."[1]

Sadi is considered a great Sufi savant by his countrymen: "No Persian writer," according to Edward G. Browne, "en-

114

joys to this day, not only in his own country, but wherever his language is cultivated, a wider celebrity or a greater reputation." His *Gulistan* (Rose Garden) and his *Bustan* (Orchard) are found in every Persian house. There is hardly a Persian-speaking man or woman who cannot recite some of Sadi's prose or poetry from memory. His odes and songs enjoy a popularity second only to those of Hafiz.[2] Although Sadi was very fluent in Arabic, expressive in Hindustani, and well-versed in Urdu, he was most eloquent in Persian.

Musharrif ud-din Ibn Muslihud-din Sadi was born in Shiraz in 1184 and died in 1291. He lost his father at an early age:

> Full well I know the pains that orphans bear,
> For as a child I lost my father's care.[3]

After receiving his early education in Shiraz, he traveled to Baghdad and entered the famous Nizamieh University where he studied under Abdul Gader Jilani, the great Sufi mentor and teacher. According to a story in *Gulistan* he accompanied his master on a pilgrimage to Mecca.

Having completed his studies, Sadi visited Asia Minor, Syria, Lebanon, Palestine, India, Turkestan, North Africa, Arabia, and Ethiopia. He traveled in true dervish fashion and mixed with all kinds of people. About 1229 he was taken prisoner by the crusaders. Referring to this incident in *Gulistan*, he wrote:

> Having become tired of my friends in Damascus, I fled to the desert of Jerusalem enjoying the company of animals until I was captured by the Franks (Crusaders) who put me to work with the Jews digging trenches. A leading citizen of Aleppo with whom I had been formerly acquainted recognized me and exclaimed: 'What has happened to you?' I answered:

'I fled from men to mountains and plain,
For I had nothing from mankind to gain;
How is my case? regard me in this den,
When I must sweat for men that are not men.
Better to hang in chain, when friends are there,
Than dwell with strangers in a garden fair.'[4]

He took pity on me and ransomed me for ten dinars
from the captivity of the Franks. Then he took me to
Aleppo where he forced me to marry his daughter, with a
dowry of one hundred dinars. After a while she became
ill-tempered, quarrelsome, disobedient, and abusive:

A bad wife comes with a good man to dwell;
She soon converts his present world to hell.
Beware of evil partnership, beware—
From hellish torment, Lord, thy servants spare.

Once in a torrent of abuse she said, 'Are you not that
man whom my father bought back from the Franks?' I
said, 'Yes, I am that man whom he bought back from the
Frankish chains for ten dinars, and delivered into your
bondage for a hundred dinars.'

Bustan, Sadi's first composition, probably was finished
about 1257. This book along with *Gulistan* enjoys a popularity unprecedented in Persian literature. Many verses from
Bustan and *Gulistan* are quoted as proverbs and anecdotes
by Persian-speaking people. "The interweaving of popular
wisdom with appropriate anecdote is done with great skill,
and Sadi also shows himself a master at telling a simple
story; the inclusion of numerous incidents from his own
adventurous life, whether true or false, or a mixture of
truth and falsehood, lends an authority and a verisimilitude
to the lessons inculcated."[5]
Ralph Waldo Emerson compares Sadi to Benjamin
Franklin:

Sadi, though he has not the lyric delights of Hafiz, has wit, practical sense, and just moral sentiments. He has the instinct to teach, and from every occurrence must draw the moral, like Franklin. He is the poet of friendship, love, self-devotion, and serenity. There is a uniform force in his page, and, conspicuously, a tone of cheerfulness which has almost made his name a synonym for this grace. The trait is no result of levity, much less of convivial habit, but first of a happy nature, to which victory is habitual, easily shedding mishap. . . . He inspires in the reader a good hope.[6]

Sir William Jones, whose translation of Sadi's quatrains won the esteem and interest of many English-speaking people, compares Sadi with Pope and Dryden.

Sadi's works are a collection of love poems, mystical stories and proverbs, advice and admonition, contradictory ethical and moral statements, commendation and condemnation of kings and potentates, lurid and even erotic stories. "Indeed," comments Edward Browne, "the real charm of Sadi and the secret of his popularity lies not in his consistency but in his catholicity; in his works is matter for every taste, the highest and lowest, the most refined and the most coarse, and from his pages sentiments may be called worthy on the one hand of Ekhardt or Thomas a Kempis, or on the other of Caesar Borgia and Heliogabalus."[7]

Sadi belongs to that group of Persian Sufi poets that tantalize readers by keeping them, as it were, suspended between matter and spirit. Nearly every line of this group is a play of wit. Lovers, beloved, taverns, wine, beauty, and women are painted with most elegant and alluring colors but with such cleverness and ambiguity that often the same poem will enchant the sinner and entrance the saint.

Some will have it that the wine in all the Sufi poems was the wine of the spirit, and that the love was the love of God.

This may be true of some Sufi poets like Rumi, Shabastari, and Jami. But to interpret the masterpieces of all the great Sufi poets, who were human beings with tender feelings and passions, in this fashion is to ignore the reality of life. In the works of these poets there is little lasciviousness, and no impure feeling darkens natural pleasure. Emotions and sense, body and soul, are here made finally and equally happy in a single experience.

All that the Sufi poets say bears the stamp of genius. When they speak, it is as if a higher spirit gave utterance through them, as it did through the prophets, communicating superhuman truth in human fashion.

Goethe describes such inspiration:

> Thus myself, myself was not,
> And a God through me did speak
> When I do speak did I think:
> And when I through a deity spoke,
> 'Twas I myself.[8]

3

Sadi's writings mirror his time showing its noblest and its most ignoble aspects. In the following verses, Sadi's concern for the plight of the orphan is expressed:

Protect thou the orphan whose father is dead;
Brush the mud from his dress, ward all hurt from his head.
Thou know'st not how hard his condition must be:
When the root has been cut, is there life in thee?
Caress not and kiss not a child of thine own
In the sight of an orphan neglected and alone.

If the orphan sheds tears, who his grief will assuage?
If his temper should fail him, who cares for his rage?

O see that he weep not, for surely God's throne

Doth quake at the orphan's most pitiful moan.
With infinite pity, with tenderest care,
Wipe the tears from his eyes, brush the dust from his hair.
The sorrows of orphans full well can I share,
Since I tasted in childhood the orphan's despair.[9]

Sadi's sense of universalism and his humanitarian sentiments are defined in the following verses:

All Adam's sons are limbs of one another,
Each of the selfsame substance as his brother:
So, while one member suffers ache and grief,
The other members cannot win relief.
Thou, who are heedless of thy brother's pain,
It is not right at all to name thee Man.[10]

Later, he extends this sense of universalism beyond the human race:

Crush not yon ant, who stores the golden grain:
He lives with pleasure, and will die with pain:
Learn from him rather to secure the spoil
Of patient cares and persevering toil.[11]

As spokesman for the poor, he reminds kings of their responsibilities:

Kings are but guardians who the poor should keep,
Though this world's goods wait on their diadem.
Not for the shepherd's welfare are the sheep;
The shepherd, rather, is for pasturing them.
Today thou markest one flushed with success,
Another sick with struggle against fate;
Pause but a little while, the earth shall press
His brain that did such plans erst meditate.
Lost is the difference of king and slave
At the approach of destiny's decree;
Should one upturn the ashes of the grave,

Could he discern 'twixt wealth and poverty?
Wealth, fame, power, fate, favor, time, youth, and beauty,
All are subject to change but eternal love.[12]

Although Sadi had kings and potentates as his patrons,
yet he was suspicious and contemptuous of them. In *Gulistan* he narrates the story of a certain minister who, having
been dismissed from office, joined the rank of dervishes.
After a while when the King wished to reinstate him in
office, he firmly declined the honor. "But," said the King, "I
need a competent and wise man to direct the affairs of the
state." "Then," retorted the ex-minister, "you will not find
him, for any man possessing these qualities will refuse to
enter your service."

"Wise men have said that one ought to be much on one's
guard against the fickle nature of kings, who will at one time
take offense at a salutation and at another bestow honors in
return for abuse."[13]

Talking to the Shah of Persia, Sadi declared: "A Shah
must practice justice that they may gather around him, and
clemency, that they may dwell in safety under the shadow of
his government; but you possess neither of these qualities."

A tyrannic man cannot be a king
As a wolf cannot be a shepherd;
A shah who establishes oppression
Destroys the basis of the wall of his own reign.[14]

A king who allows his subjects to be oppressed
Will in his day of calamity become a violent foe.
Be at peace with subjects and sit safe from attacks of foe.
Because his subjects are the army of a just king.
With a powerful arm and the strength of the wrist
    to break the five fingers of a poor man is sin.
Let him be afraid who spares not the fallen,
Because if he falls no one will take hold of his hand.

Whoever sows bad seed and expects good fruit
Has cudgeled his brains for nought and begotten vain im-
  aginations.
Extract the cotton from thy ears and administer justice to
  thy people
And if thou failest to do so, there is a day of retribution.[15]

  O tyrant, who oppressest thy subjects,
  How long wilt thou persevere in this?
  Of what use is authority to thee?
  To die is better for thee than to oppress men.

  If the king eats one apple from the garden of a subject
  His soldiers will pull up all the trees from the roots.

  A tyrant does not remain in the world
  But the curse on him abides forever.

  If livelihood were dependent on knowledge
  None would be more needy than the ignorant.
  Nevertheless the ignorant receive a livelihood
  At which the learned stand aghast.
  The luck of wealth consists not in skill.
  But only in the aid of heaven.
  It happens in the world that many
  Silly men are honored and sages despised.
  If an alchemist has died in grief and misery
  A fool discovered a treasure amidst ruins.[16]

  Sadi was very critical of kings who neglected the affairs of
their countries and seldom concerned themselves with the
welfare of their subjects:

  I have heard that Darius of fortunate race
  Got detached from his suite, on the day of the chase.
  Before him came running a horse-tending lout;
  The king from his quiver an arrow pulled out,
  In the desert 'tis well to show terror of foes,
  For at home not a thorn will appear on the rose;

The terrified horse-keeper uttered a cry,
Saying: "Do not destroy me! no foeman am I.
I am he who takes care of the steeds of the king;
In this meadow, with zeal to my duty I cling."
The king's startled heart found composure again;
He smiled and exclaimed: "Oh most foolish of men!
Some fortunate angel has succored you here;
Else the string of my bow I'd have brought to my ear."

The guard of the pasturage smiled and replied:
"Admonition from friends it becomes not to hide,
The arrangements are bad and the counsels unwise,
When the king can't a friend from a foe recognize.
The condition of living in greatness is so,
That every dependent you have you should know.
You often have seen me when present at court,
And inquired about horses and pastures and sport,
And now that in love I have met you again,
Me you cannot distinguish from rancorous men.
As for me, I am able, oh name-bearing king!
Any horse out of one hundred thousand to bring.
With wisdom and judgment as herdsman I serve;
Do you in like manner your own flock preserve!"
In that capital anarchy causes distress,
Where the plans of the king than the herdsman's are less.[17]

Sadi's poems have a message of advice for both princes
and paupers:

A disciple without purpose is a lover without money:
A traveller without knowledge is a bird without wings;
A scholar without practice is a tree without fruit;
A devotee without education is a house without a door.
A good-humored and pleasant military officer is superior to
   a theologian who hurts people.
An educated man without practice resembles a bee without
   honey.

An avaricious ruler is a highway robber.

Vinegar by one's own labor and crumbs of bread are better than food received through charity without working for it.

You learn by not being ashamed to ask about things you do not know.

Ask what thou knowest not; for the trouble of asking will indicate to the way of the dignity of knowledge.

Who interrupts the conversation of others, that they may know his excellence, they will become acquainted only with the degree of his folly.

Gold is obtained from a mine by digging it, but from a miser by taking his life.

Who has no compassion and sympathy for inferiors
Will suffer from the tyranny of superiors.

O, Lord, have mercy upon the wicked, because thou hast already had mercy upon decent men by creating and giving them strength to be decent.

When you have to give away what belongs to others, give it with grace and dignity. If you do not pay your tax of your own accord, the tax collector will take it by force.

What can an old prostitute do but to vow to become chaste, and a deposed ruler not to commit oppression upon men?

> To adorn oneself with one's own rag
> Is better than to ask for the royal robe.

The noblest of beings is evidently man, and the meanest a dog; but intelligent persons agree that a grateful dog is better than an ungrateful man. A dog never forgets a morsel received, though thou throwest a stone at him a hundred times. But if thou cherishest a mean fellow a lifetime, he will for a trifle suddenly turn against thee.[18]

> The sinner's bleeding heart in anguish sighs,
> The saint upon his piety relies,

Doth he not know that God resisteth pride,
But takes the low in spirit to His side?
Whose heart is vile, but outside fair to see,
For him hell's gates yawn wide, he wants no key,
Humility in His sight is more meet
Than strict religious forms and self-conceit!
Thy self-esteem but proves how bad thou art,
For egotism with God can have no part,
Boast not thyself—however swift his pace,
Not every skillful rider wins the race.
Wise men have left for all this saying true,
And Sadi in this tale remindeth you,
The sinner penitent hath less to fear
Than he whose piety is not sincere.[19]

Sadi believes in human dignity and feels that no matter
how low or humble people are, there is a place and price for
their ability. He resents arrogance, hates oppression, and
condemns cruelty and the inhumanity of kings and rulers.

From the cloud there descended a drop of rain;
'Twas ashamed when it saw the expanse of the main,
Saying, "Who may I be, where the sea has its run?
If the sea has existence, I truly, have none."

Since in its own eyes the drop humble appeared;
In its bosom, a shell with its life the drop reared;
The sky brought the work with success to a close,
And a famed royal pearl from the raindrop arose.
Because it was humble it excellence gained;
Patiently waiting till success was obtained.[20]

Oh, sensible person. In silence serene
You have honor, and people unworthy, a screen.
If you have learning, you should not your dignity lose.
If you are ignorant, tear not the curtain you use.
The beasts are all dumb, and man's tongue is released;
A nonsensical talker is worse than a beast;

A speaker should talk in a sensible strain;
If he can't; like the brutes, he should silence maintain.[21]

Straightness is the means of acceptance with God,
I saw no one lost on the straight road.

In the sea there are countless gains,
But if thou desirest safety, it will be on the shore.

Account him not a friend who knocks at the door of pros-
    perity
Boasts of amity and calls himself thy adopted brother.
I consider him a friend who takes a friend's hands
When he is in distressed state and in poverty.

Knowest thou not that thou wilt see thy feet in bonds
If the advice of people cannot penetrate into thy ear?

Oxen and asses who carry loads
Are superior to men oppressing mankind.

A tyrant does not remain in the world
But the curse on him abides forever.

If thou desirest peace from the foe, whenever he
Finds fault behind thy back praise him to his face,
A vicious fellow's mouth must utter words.
If thou desirest not bitter words, sweeten his mouth.

Beware of the bitterness of internal wounds
Because at last an internal wound will break out.
Forbear to uproot one heart as long as thou canst
Because one sigh may uproot a world.

Either fidelity itself does not exist in this world
Or nobody practices it in our time.
No one had learnt archery from me
Without at last making a target of me.

My God (Friend) is nearer to me than myself,

But it is more strange that I am far from Him.
What am I to do? To whom can it be said that He
Is in my arms, but I am exiled from Him.[22]

Sadi admonishes leaders who never practice what they
preach:

They teach people to abandon the world
But themselves accumulate silver and gold.
A scholar who only preaches and nothing more
Will not impress anyone when he speaks.
He is a scholar who commits no evil,
Not he who speaks to men but acts not himself.[23]

Sadi was also a social reformer who hoped that a just
distribution of wealth would save the world from violent
revolution. But he abhorred laziness and begging:
"A Western supplicant, addressing a group in the market
place of Aleppo, stated: 'Lords of wealth, if you were just
and fain and we contented and grateful, poverty would
vanish from the surface of the world.' "

Who eats bread by the work of his own hand.
Will not bear to be obliged to Hatim Tai.

Who opens to himself a door for begging
Will till he dies remain a needy fellow.
Abandon greediness and be a king
Because a head without greed is high.[24]

Sadi believed that graciousness, patience, and courtesy
were the essential attributes of every decent human being:
"Galenus saw a fool hanging on with his hands to the
collar of a learned man and insulting him, whereon he said:
'If he were learned he would not be involved with a fool.' "

4

Why have Sadi's works become so popular and successful? The answer to this question can be found in the fact that in Sadi there is something for everybody. The work is simple but subtle, didactic but entertaining, delightful and delicate: in sum, an exquisite piece of art. "Few things in *Gulistan* could be stigmatized as too heavy, or too long, monotonous or patronizing—a claim that would be difficult to make in all honesty for many of Sadi's predecessors."[25]

In *Gulistan* Sadi tried to show the best and the worst of his time. During his long life, Sadi witnessed two Mongol invasions, civil wars, dynastic feuds, and the decline of Baghdad as the center of Islamic civilization, power and culture.[26] Ostensibly *Gulistan's* inconsistencies and contradictions represent the difficulties and complexities of human customs, behavior, and nature. Referring to these factors, Sadi declares:

Man's state is that of changing lightning
One moment it appears and at another vanishes.
We are sometimes sitting in high heaven:
On other occasions we cannot see the back of our foot.
Were a Sufi always to remain in the state of grace
He would desire the pleasures of neither this nor
    the next world.[27]

While there are many ethical stories and spiritual statements in *Gulistan*, the chapter on "Love and Youth" shocked and puzzled many traditional Muslims and Victorian readers. Modern observers are not likely to label it indecent or vulgar, for one may find some interesting social values in every story.

Sadi is the first Persian poet to speak of sex and love openly and frankly. The thirteenth-century Islamic world was dominated by taboos and restrictions on speech and knowledge about sex. Most Persian poets dealt with the problem of love in general and in the abstract. The lack of association and contact between male and female before marriage forced men and women to postpone, delay, and subjugate their natural sexual emotion, thereby encouraging the practice of homosexuality. To Persian society, influenced and dominated by the Mongols, marriage was an abstraction: a form of legalized cohabitation. Polygamy was very common. Divorce was easy, and the right of the husband.

Religious preachers and poets tried to dissociate love from sex, the former being God's business, the latter being the devil's. The Mongol savages were unwilling to accept ascetic ideals and saw nothing wrong in sex nor any reason to refrain from it. The sex life of the Mongol rulers and their court in the thirteenth century was grossly sensual, lustful, harsh, and vulgar. One of the Mongol rulers of Mazandaran married a Persian princess. Shortly after their marriage, he told his wife that since he was pleased with her he would be happy to do her any favor. She asked her spouse to find a good husband for her sister. The Mongol ruler instantly went to the sister-in-law's village, married her, and then returned to his wife, telling her: "I tried to find a wealthy and powerful husband for your sister, but I found none better than myself."

The status of women under the Mongols was one of degradation. They were treated like chattels and lost their position as real persons in the eyes of the law. Women were excluded from the courts, barred from inheritance and even kept out of family councils. Adultery in a wife was punishable by death; for men there was no penalty whatever.

Even the clergy, who were supposed to lead, guide, and rise above the sordid lusts of the savage rulers, clearly showed the effects of the fusion of barbarian immorality by their hypocritical words and acts.

Through stories, anecdotes, and parables, Sadi tried to describe this world of chaos, confusion, and decadence for posterity. The moral of the very first story in the *Gulistan* is that "a lie assisting people is preferable to a mischievous truth." He both condemns and condones homosexuality:

> If a Tartar slays that Sodomite
> The Tartar must not be slain in return.
> How long will he be like the bridge of Baghdad,
> With water flowing beneath and men on the back?[28]

Despite this statement, in another story he confesses: "In the exuberance of youth, as it usually happens, I was on the closest terms of intimacy with a sweetheart who had a melodious voice and a face beautiful like the full moon.

"I asked one of the people of Baghdad what he thought of beardless youths. He replied: 'There is no good in them, for when one of them is young and pretty and desirable, he is insolent; but when he becomes older and he is no more needed he becomes affable.' "

> When a beardless youth is beautiful and sweet
> His speech is bitter, his temper hasty.
> When his beard grows and he attains puberty,
> He associates with men and seeks affection.[29]

The following story from *Gulistan* is a sad reflection on the moral decadence of Sadi's era:

"It is related that the judge of the city of Hamadan, having conceived affection towards a farrier-boy, sought for some time to meet him, roaming about and seeking for opportunities to meet him.

"I was informed that the boy, who had heard something

of the judge's passion, happening to meet him in a
thoroughfare, manifested immense wrath, assailed the
judge with disrespectful and insulting words, snatched up a
stone and left no injury untried. The judge, in a philosophical mood, murmured an Arabic proverb:

> "A slap from a lover is as sweet as a raisin.
> A blow from thy hand on the mouth
> Is sweeter than eating sweets with one's own hand."

After saying these words, the judge returned to his court
where some prominent members of the community met
with him and said that although it would not be polite to
find fault with such a great man, it was beneath the dignity
of his lordship to surrender to his desires concerning this
boy. They implored him to put an end to his lascivious
desire and save the good reputation and honor of his sublime office:

> One who has done many disreputable things
> Cares nothing for the reputation of anyone.
> But many a good name of fifty years
> Was trodden underfoot by one imprudent act.

The judge, listening to the admonition of his friends and
appreciating their sincere loyalty, said that their view was
quite right; nevertheless, nothing could overcome his fond-
ness and love for the youth. He then sent some of his men
to find the farrier-boy, instructing them to spend unlimited
sums of money, because whoever has gold in his hand has
power and he who is devoid of gold has neither power nor
friends in this world.

One night the police obtained information that the judge
was in a palace with his sweetheart enjoying wine and singing:

Had this cock perhaps not crowed at the proper time
  This night
And have the lovers not had their fill of embrace, and kiss
Whilst alas for only a moment the eye of confusion is
  asleep?
Remain awake that life may not elapse in vain.

While the judge was in this state one of his friends entered and said: "Arise and run as fast as you can, because
your enemies and the envious have seized on this unfortu-
nate situation and they are conspiring for your downfall."
The judge, however, replied:

"When the lion has his claws in the game
What boots it if a jackal makes his appearance?
Keep thy face on the face of the friend and leave
The foe to chew the back of his own hand in rage."

The same night the king, informed of the situation, was
asked what he thought of it. He replied that the judge was
one of the most learned men and a paragon of virtue. Since
his enemies might have devised a plot against the judge, he
would believe nothing he had not witnessed personally:

"He who grasps the sword in haste
Will, repenting, carry the back of his hand to his teeth and
  bite it."

At dawn, the king arrived at the house of the judge and
saw the sweetheart sitting, the wine spilled, the goblet broken and the judge plunged in the sleep of drunkenness,
unaware of the world and its problems. The king awakened
him gently and said: "Get up, for the sun has risen." The
judge, realizing his serious situation, asked: "From what
direction?" The astonished sultan replied: "From the east,
as usual." The judge exclaimed: "Praise to Allah! The door

of repentance is yet open, because, according to the
prophet, the gate of repentance will not be locked against
worshippers till the sun rises from the west."

"Two things led me to sin
My ill star and my imperfect and frivolous nature.
If thou givest me punishment I deserve it.
And if thou pardon me, forgiveness is sweeter than re-
venge."

The king replied:

"What is the use to promise to forego thieving
When a lasso cannot be thrown up to the palace?
Say to the tall man: Do not pluck the fruit
For he who is short cannot reach the branch."

"Thou hast adduced this wonderful sally," the king continued, "and hast encouraged a strange maxim, but it is
impossible according to reason and custom that you should
be saved from the punishment which I have decreed; and I
consider it proper to throw thee headlong from the palace
so that others may take example." The judge pleaded: "O
Lord of the world, I have been favored by the magnanimity
of this dynasty, and I am not the first sinner in this world.
Throw another man headlong that I may learn my lesson
for the future." The king burst into laughter, pardoned the
judge, and said to his courtiers who were waiting for the
death of the judge:

"All of you who are saddled with your own faults
Should never blame others for their defects."[30]

Sadi was married twice. His remarks concerning women
are contradictory. They are caustic, cynical, and unflatter-
ing, but at the same time warm and laudatory:

Bid farewell to pleasure in a house
Where the shouting of a woman is loud.
A wife who is charming, obedient, and chaste,
Makes a king of the man knowing poverty's taste.
Go! And boast by the beat of five drums at your gate.
That you have by your side an agreeable mate!
If, by day, sorrow trouble you, be not distressed!
When, by night, a grief-soother reclines on your breast!
When a man's house is thriving, his wife friendly too,
Towards him is directed God's merciful view.
When a lovely-faced woman is modest and nice,
Her husband on seeing her tastes paradise.
The man in this world his heart's longing has found,
Whose wife and himself are in harmony bound.
If choice in her language and chaste in her ways,
On her beauty or ugliness fix not your gaze!
For the heart by an amiable wife's more impressed,
Than by one of great personal beauty possessed;
A sociable nature is hostile to strife.
And covers a number of faults in a wife.
An agreeable wife is a joy to the heart,
But, O God! From a wicked one keep me apart.

Oh friend! Take a bride every spring that ensues!
For a past season's almanac no one will use.
Better barefooted walk than in tight shoes to roam;
Better travel's misfortune than fighting at home.
Some wives are tyrannical, headstrong, and bold,
But are pleased when they share your embrace, I am told.
Oh Sadi! Do not jeer at his life!
When you see that a man is henpecked by his wife.
You, too, are oppressed and her load you abide,
If once you invite her to come to your side.[31]

Sadi states that the most significant thing for a woman is love: "What is it that love does to a woman? Without it she only sleeps; with it, alone, she lives." But he also mentions the importance of sexual satisfaction:

A woman who arises without satisfaction from a man
Will raise many a quarrel and contention.
An old man who is unable to rise from his place,
Except by the aid of a stick, how can his own organ rise?

Sadi believed that young girls prefer headstrong, rough,
fickle-minded and unfaithful young men to generous, gentle, and kind old men:

Despite of all his violence and hasty nature
I shall try to please thee because thou art young.
To be with thee in hell burning is for me
Better than to be with the other in paradise.
The smell of an onion from the mouth of a pretty face
Is indeed better than a rose from an ugly hand.
A nice face and a gown of gold brocade,
Essence of roses, fragrant aloes, paint, perfume, and lust:
All these are ornaments of women.
For a man; his phallus and testicles are sufficient orna-
    ments.

> Let not a man of seventy years make love,
> Thou art confessedly blind, kiss her and sleep,
> The lady wants virility, not gold.[32]

Sadi believed that true love conquers all things.

A handsome woman is a jewel; a good woman is a treasure.
A virtuous and beauteous youth
Was pledged to a chaste maiden.
I read that in the great sea
They fell into a vortex together.
When a sailor came to take his hand,
Lest he might die in that condition,
He said in anguish from the waves:
"Leave me. Take the hand of my love."

> Whilst saying this, he despaired of life.
> In his agony he was heard to exclaim:

"Learn not the tale of love from the wretch
Who forgets his beloved in distress."
Thus the lives of the lovers terminated.

Learn from what has occurred that thou mayest know
Because Sadi is one of the ways and means of love affairs
Well aware in the Arabian city of Baghdad.
Tie the heart to the heart-charmer thou possessed
And shut thy eye to all the rest of the world.
If Majnun and Laili were to come to life again
They might indite a tale of love on this occurrence.[33]

Fortune suffers me not to clasp my sweetheart to my breast,
Nor lets me forget my exile long in a kiss on her sweet lip
  pressed.
The noose wherewith she is wont to snare her victims far
  and wide
I will steal away, that so one day I may lure her to my side.
Yet I shall not dare caress her hair with a hand that is
  overbold,
For snared therein, like birds in a gin, are the hearts of
  lovers untold.

A slave am I to that gracious form, which, as I picture it,
Is clothed in grace with a measuring-rod, as tailors a garment fit.
Old cypress-tree, with silver limbs, this colour and scent of
  thine
Have shamed the scent of the myrtle-plant and the bloom
  of the eglantine.

Judge with thine eyes, and set thy foot in the garden fair
  and free,
And tread the jasmine under thy foot, and the flowers of
  the Judas-tree.

Lover's souls begin to dance with glee
When the zephyr fans thy roses.
Never melts thy stony heart for me,

Mine as a sunk stone heavily
In thy dimple's well reposes.

Life were an offering too small,
Else 'tis easy to surrender
Unto thee, who need'st not call
Painter's art to deck thy wall:
Thou alone dost give it splendor.

Better sicken, better die
At thy feet than live to lose thee.
Pilgrim to love's sanctuary,
What car'st thou, 'neath desert sky,
How the thorns of absence bruise thee?[34]

Look now, the Lord's sweet charity.
His servant sins, ashamed is He.
Better set, dumb and deaf aside
Than wag a tongue thou can'st not guide.

The heart that loves with patience—a stone—is not a heart;
Nay, love and patience dwell of old a thousand leagues
    apart.
O Brethren of the mystic path, leave blame and me alone.
Repentance in the way of Love is glass against a stone.
No more in secret need I drink, in secret dance and sing,
For us that love religiously, good name's a shameful thing.
What right and justice should I see or what instructions
    hear?
Mine eye is to the Saqi (the cupbearer) turned, and to the
    lute mine ear
Who'll bring a message to my dear that off in anger went?
Go, tell Him I have dropped the shield if He on war is bent;
And let him kill as He knows how. For if no vision there be
Of Him, the wide world seems a cramped uneasy place to
    me.[35]

O cameleer, drive gently now. My soul's delight is fain to
    flee,
And takes away with her the heart which I before kept safe
    with me.

Here I remain unblest by her, despairing and distressed by
    her;
Methinks, a lancet pressed by her both pierce my bones,
    tho' far she be.
"With many a charm and spell," I cried, "this inward ulcer I
    will hide":
Lo, streaming o'er the lintel wide my blood lets out the
    mystery.
My beloved departed in disdain and left me to a life of pain,
Dark fumes are mounting from my brain: like coals of fire I
    burn, ah me.

With all her cruelty and scorn, her pledges vain and vows
    forsworn,
Still on my tongue her name is borne, and in my breast her
    memory.
Hold back the howdahs, camel-man. Chide not the tardy
    caravan:
I soar beyond mine earthly span for love of that fair cypress
    tree.[36]

But Sadi writes not only of romantic love:

We are intoxicated by the pure wine of spiritual love:
We do not thirst for the water of paradise. I, as well
as the heart-sick wakeful lover, can appreciate the
prolongation of the long, dark night.
To outward appearance thou art not near us, but thou
art never remote from our mind's eye.

Arise and let us keep the vow of fidelity to "our trust"
and atone for our past sins by means of service.
It was an act of folly on our part to humble ourselves
before men: henceforth let us practice humility at the
door of Divine Majesty.

Let us put aside lust and desire and heart's vain passions:
Let us bend double the back of devotion with a single heart,
It is a pity that the hearts of men should get into the
power of the Devil, how long shall we surrender the home
of the friend to the enemy?

Set not thy heart exclusively on any land or friend,
For lands and seas are countless, and sweethearts without
end.

   Sadi believed that mothers were the holiest creations of
God. They were the sweet rallying point for affection,
obedience, dedication, devotion, and tenderness. His story
concerning his own mother shows the depth of his attach-
ment and affection for her:
   "In the folly of youth I one day shouted at my mother,
who then sat down with a grieved heart in a corner and
said, weeping: 'Hast thou forgotten thy infancy that thou
art harsh towards me?' "

How sweetly said the old women to her son
When she saw him overthrow a tiger, and elephant-bodied:
"If thou hadst remembered the time of infancy
How helpless thou wast in my arms
Thou wouldst this day not have been harsh
For thou art a lionlike man, and I an old woman."[37]

   The power of the mother, wrote Sadi, is the mightiest. It
transforms men and things by its love and self-sacrifice. It
turns cruelty into compassion, cowardice into courage,
selfishness into self-negation, thoughtlessness into consideration, pride into humility, and vanity into admiring love.
   Sadi's outlook on life was fundamentally one of open-
hearted joy and exultation. In the following poems he jus-
tifies the Sufi dance and expresses his approval of music
and songs as a part of Sufi rituals:

Do not blame the bewildered dervish:
If he waves his hands and feet, the reason is that he is
   drowning;
The dance opens a door in the soul to divine influences,
It spreads wide the hands to all things created;

The dance is good when it arises from remembrance of the
  beloved.
Then each waving sleeve has a soul in it
If you set out bravely to swim
You can best shake arms and legs when divested of cloth-
  ing:
Strip off the robes of earthly honor and hypocrisy:
A drowning man is hampered by his clothes.

I will not say, my brother, what song is
Before I know who the listener is.
If the bird has flown from the dove-cote of meaning,
Even an angel will fall short of its achievement.
If the listener is a frivolous and flippant man,
The devil in his brain is but strengthened by it.
Flowers are scattered by the morning breeze,
Wood not the axe can split that.[38]

5

Hitherto we have spoken of Sadi's *Gulistan* and *Bustan*,
but besides these two books there is his *Kollyyat*, "Collected
Works," comprising Arabic and Persian poems (*qasidas*).
The study of these poems explains some of the wide-
ranging interests of Sadi. One of these *qasidas* deals with the
destruction of Baghdad and the death of Caliph Al-
Mustasem in A.D. 1258[39]:

Well it were if from the heavens tears of blood on earth
  should flow.
For the Ruler faithful Al-Mustasem, brought so low.
If Muhammad, at the Day of Judgment from the dust thy
  head thou'st raise,
Raise it now behold the Judgment fallen on thy folk below!
Waves of blood the dainty thresholds of the palace beauties
  whelm;
While from out my heart the life-blood dyes my sleeve with
  hues of woe.

Fear vicissitudes of Fortune, fear the sphere's revolting
    change;
Who could dream that such a splendor such a fate should
    overthrow?
Raise your eyes, O ye who once upon the Holy House did
    gaze,
Watching Khans and Roman Caesars cringing to its portals
    go.
Now upon that selfsame threshold where the Kings their
    foreheads laid,
From the children of the prophet's uncle streams of blood
    do flow.[40]

Sadi explains Divine providence and God's compassion in
the following poems:

Behold yon azure dome, the sapphire sky,
Rear in unpillar'd might its canopy!
That vast pavilion gemm'd with world of light
Whose circling glories boast a boundless flight—
And as they roll, survey man's chequered state,
And scan the destinies of mortal fate.
Here the poor sentry takes his lonely stand,
There throned in state, a monarch rules a land;
Here in the various grades of life, behold
Beggars for justice of th' imperial gold.
Here one in bootless toil breaks down his health,
There, whose vast treasury o'erflows with wealth;
Here on a mat, reclin'd a harassed frame,
There on a throne, who boasts the regal name,
Behold in clothing vile some take their stand,
While glow in silk the magnates of the land;
This in the wretchedness of want is found—
To that exhaustless treasuries abound.
This, unsuccessful, blames his hapless fate,
That gains his heart's desire, with hope elate.
One vigour braced—one breathes the helpless sigh;
One grey in years, and one in infancy.
One in religion, one in crime we meet—

One bow'd in prayer, one rob'd in dark deceit.
This, wont to bless us; that, too fiercely wrong;
This meekly bows; that dares the battle throng;
This, Lord of dignity, an empire's throne;
That, in sin's bondage, heaves the hopeless groan;
Here is enjoyment; there, embitter'd pain;
Here droops distress—there soars unbounded gain.
One, in the flow'ry garden of repose,
Another, constant mate of countless woes;
This man with riches' increase swells his store;
That scarce can rear a famish'd offspring poor.
See here, the lamp of gladness beaming bright;
There sorrow turns the fairest day to night!
Here, crowned brows—there, claim'd the tribute just;
This rears his head; that prostrates in the dust.
Here gladness reigns supreme, and there is grief;
Here boasts prosperity; there, needs relief;
These, smiling as the rose from pleasures glow;
Those, spirit wounded, deepest sorrows show.
One breathes his soul in prayer and praise sublime,
Another ends a hardened life in crime.
By day and night, this reads the sacred book;
That, drugg'd by wine, sleeps in yon tavern nook.
One as a pillar in God's temple stands:
Another joins the caffer's faithless bands.
One blest with deeds of faith and charity!
Another whelm'd in seas of infamy.
One prudent, wise, and polish'd here we find,
Another senseless, and of brutish mind;
Here the bold hero dares the mortal strife,
There flies the coward trembling for his life;
These, at the threshold of the living God;
Those, throng the infidel's abandoned road.[41]

Historians say that in the ancient days,
When Jesus walked on earth (to Him be praise!)
There lived a man so bad, so sunk in sin,
That even Satan was ashamed of him;
The Book contained his name so many times,
No room was left to enter all his crimes.

Perished his tree of life, and bore no fruit,
A stupid, cruel, drunken, swinish brute.
Hard by there dwelt a holy devotee,
Known far and wide for strictest piety;
Each was the marvel of the time and place,
The first of wickedness and this of grace.
Jesus (to Him be praise!) I've heard one day
Forth from the desert came and passed that way;
Th' recluse, descending from his casement high,
Fell at His feet with proud humility;
The lost one gazed with wonder at the sight
Like moth bewildered by the candle's light;
Surely one gentle touch had reached his heart,
From Him who came to take the sinner's part!
Shrinking with shame, his conscience stricken sore
As shrinks a beggar at a rich man's door,
Tears of repentance rolling down his face,
For days and nights polluted with disgrace,
With fear and hope, God's mercy to invoke,
In earnest prayer, with bated breath he spoke:
"My precious life I've wasted day by day,
My opportunities I've thrown away;
In vice and wickedness surpassed by none,
No single act of goodness have I done;
Would that like me no mortal e'er might be,
Better by far to die than live like me!
He who in childhood dies is free from blame,
Old age comes not to bow his head with shame
Forgive my sins, Creator of the world,
Lest I to blackest depths of hell be hurled."

On that side, lo! the aged sinner cries,
Not daring heavenward to lift his eyes,
Repentant, weeping, sunk in deep despair;
"Help of the helpless! hear, oh! hear my prayer."
On this, the devotee puffed up with pride,
With visage sour from far the sinner eyed:
"What brings this ill-starred wretch towards this place,
Dares he to think himself of man's high race?

Headlong to fire eternal he has fallen,
His life to lust's foul whirlwind he has given,
His sin-stained soul what good can show that he
Messiah's company should share with me!
I loathe his hateful countenance, and dread
Lest sin's infection to my bosom spread;
In that great day, when all must present be,
O God! I pray Thee, raise him not with me."
From the all-glorious God a message came
To Jesus (ever blessed be His name!):
"The ignorant and learned both are saved,
Both I accept since both to me have prayed;
The lost one, humbled, with repentant tears
Has cried to me, his cry has reached my ears;
Who helpless lowly seeks, and doth not doubt
The mercy seat, shall never be cast out;
His many wicked deeds I have forgiven,
My boundless mercy bringeth him to heaven;
And should the devotee on that great day
Think it disgrace in heaven with him to stay,
Tell him, Beware! they take thee not to hell
And him to paradise with God to dwell."

The sinner's bleeding heart in anguish sighs,
The saint upon his piety relies,
Doth he not know that God resisteth pride,
But takes the low in spirit to His side?
Whose heart is vile, but outside fair to see,
For him hell's gates yawn wide, he wants no key,
Humility in His sight is more meet
Than strict religious forms and self-conceit;
Thy self-esteem but proves how bad thou art,
For egotism with God can have no part;
Boast not thyself—however swift his pace,
Not every skilful rider wins the race.
Wise men have left for all this saying true,
And Sa'di in this tale remindeth you,
The sinner penitent hath less to fear
Than he whose piety is not sincere.[42]

Sadi expressed both pleasure and displeasure in his native city of Shiraz:

O joyous and gay is the New Year's Day, and in Shiraz most
    of all;
Even the stranger forgets his home and becomes its willing
    thrall.
O'er the garden's Egypt, Joseph-like, the fair red-rose is
    King.
And the zephyr, e'en to the heart of the town doth the scent
    of his raiment bring.
O wonder not if in time of spring thou dost rouse such
    jealousy,
That the cloud doth weep while the flowers smile, and all on
    account of thee! [43]

When Sadi fell from favor at the court, he considered for a time leaving the city of Shiraz and seeking his fortune in Baghdad:

My soul is weary of Shiraz, utterly sick and sad
If you seek for news of my doings, you will have to ask at
    Baghdad.
I have no doubt that the premier there will give me the help
    I need;
Should the help refuse to one like me, I should deem it
    strange indeed!
Sadi, that love of one's native land is a true tradition is
    clear! [44]
But I cannot afford to die of want because my birth was
    here. [45]

Sadi's odes (*Ghazals*) in beauty and popularity are second to no Persian poet's, including the king of odes, Hafiz of Shiraz:

When the enemy doth throw
    His lasso,

As his whim determines, so
  We must do.

None has earned, till he has loved,
  Manly fame,
E'en as silver pure is proved
  By the flame.

Never did reformer take
  Passion's way,
But that both worlds he must stake
  In the play.

To his memory I am so
  Wholly turned,
That with self my mind is no
  More concerned.

Thanks to love sincere and whole
  I confess;
Love, that burned my heart, my soul
  Doth caress.

Sadi! poet sweeter page
  Never writ
For a present to an age
  Great with wit.

May thy sugar tongue remain
  Ever blest,
That hath taught the world such pain
  And unrest.[46]

Roses are blossoming
And joyous birds do sing
In such a season gay,
A desert-faring day.

Autumn the scatterer
Setteth the leaves astir;

The painter morning air
Decketh the garden fair.

Yet no desire have I
In grassy meads to lie;
Where'er thou art in sight,
There dwelleth true delight.

Beauty to view, they said,
Is joy prohibited:
Nay, but our view of bliss
Lawful and holy is.

Lo, in thy face I see
Creation's mystery,
As water doth appear
Within a crystal clear.

Whatever man thy love
Seals not his heart above,
No heart is his to own
But flint, and granite stone.

These flames (one of these days)
That 'neath the cauldron blaze
Will burn me utterly
And make an end of me.

Sadi's distressful dole
And tears uncountable
(They say) are contrary
To all propriety.

They say; but little those
Who on the shore repose
Know of the woe that we
Bear on the stormy sea.[47]

1. Introduction to Sadi's *The Gulistan*, trans. Edward Rehatsek, George Allen and Unwin Ltd., London, 1964, p. 17.
2. E. G. Browne, *A Literary History of Persia*, vol. II, Fisher, Unwin, London, 1906, pp. 525–526.

Sadi of Shiraz, the Wisdom of Sufism   147

3. Arberry, A. J., *Shiraz, Persian City of Saints and Poets*, University of Oklahoma Press, 1960, p. 114.
4. Sadi, *Gulistan*, Chapter II, Story 81, translated by A. J. Arberry.
5. *Ibid.*, p. 196.
6. *The Works of Ralph Waldo Emerson*, Tudor Publishing Co., New York, p. 184.
7. E. G. Browne, *op. cit.*, pp. 530–32.
8. Victor Karl Goethe, *The Poet*, Harvard University Press, 1947, p. 24.
9. Sadi, *Bustan*, translated by E. G. Browne.
10. Sadi, *Gulistan*, *op. cit.*
11. *Bustan*, translated by Sir William Jones.
12. Sadi, *Gulistan*, translated by E. B. Eastwick.
13. Sadi, *Gulistan*, *op. cit.*, p. 237.
14. *Ibid.*, p. 82.
15. *Ibid.*, p. 85.
16. *Ibid.*, p. 111.
17. A. Elizabeth Reed, *Persian Literature*, Chicago, S. C. Griggs & Company, 1893, pp. 316–17.
18. Sadi, *Gulistan*, translated by E. Rehatsek and the author.
19. Sadi, *Kullyat*, Teheran Press, p. 65. translated by W. C. MacKinnen.
20. Reed, *Persian Literature*, *op. cit.*, p. 312.
21. *Ibid.*, p. 315.
22. *Ibid.*
23. *Ibid.*
24. *Ibid.*
25. *Ibid.*
26. Baghdad was sacked by Hulagu, the Mongol ruler, in 1257.
27. Sadi, *Gulistan*, translated by the author.
28. *Ibid.*
29. *Ibid.*
30. Sadi, *Gulistan*, translated by Edward Rehatsek and the author, pp. 199–204.
31. Sadi, *Bustan*, trans. George Scott Davie, Teheran Press, pp. 162–63.
32. *Ibid.*
33. Sadi's *Gulistan*, *op. cit.*, p. 204.
34. Sadi, *Gulistan*, translated by R. A. Nicholson.
35. *Ibid.*
36. Browne, *op. cit.*
37. Sadi, *Gulistan*, *op. cit.*, p. 210.
38. Cyprian Rice, *The Persian Sufis*, George Allen and Unwin Ltd., London, 1964, p. 22.
39. The ancestors of Mustasem, the Abbasside Caliphs were cousins of the Prophet Muhammad.
40. Browne, *op. cit.*, vol. II, pp. 29–30.
41. E. Pocock, *Persian Poems*, edited by A. J. Arberry, J. M. Dent & Sons, Ltd., London, 1964, pp. 129–30.
42. *Ibid.*, pp. 54–55.
43. *Sadi*, translated by E. G. Browne.
44. The tradition mentioned by Sadi comes from an Arabic proverb: "Patriotism is a part of faith."
45. Browne, *op. cit.*, p. 536.
46. A. J. Arberry, *Persian Poems*, *op. cit.*, p. 53.
47. *Ibid.*, pp. 54–55.

7

Hafiz, Poet of Sufism

Learn from yon orient shell to love thy foe,
And store with pearls the hand, that bring thee woe;
Free, like yon rock, from base vindictive pride,
Emblaze with gems the wrist, that rends thy side:
Mark, where yon tree rewards the stony show'r
With fruit nectareous, or the balmy flower;
All nature calls aloud: Shall man do less
Than heal the smiter, and the railer bless?

Shams ud-din Mohammad Hafiz was born in Shiraz early in
the fourteenth century. His father having died when Hafiz
was five years old, his upbringing became the responsibility
of his mother who obtained for him the best education
available in Shiraz. As a student Hafiz distinguished himself
in Islamic philosophy and theology, in Persian and Arabic
literature, and at an early age he was recognized by his
teachers and patrons. One of the latter, Qavum ud-Din,
founded a school of theology for him in Shiraz, where Hafiz
lectured on theology and Islamic ideas. His wisdom, eloquence, and learning won him such a great reputation that

148

the titles of "Tongue of the Unseen" and "Interpreter of Mysteries" were bestowed upon him.

Shiraz, which Hafiz loved so much, was the capital of the Muzafferi Kings and a center of civil dissension and strife. But despite political vicissitudes, the state of culture in Persia was so high and Hafiz's fame so widespread that he was held in respect and honor by all the feuding parties.

Little is known of Hafiz's personal life beyond a few traditional stories connected with certain verses of his poems, and the anecdotes of some of his contemporary poets. We gather from the two following tender poems that Hafiz was married to a girl by the name of Shakh Nabat (crystal sugar) and had a son, both of whom he lost in his youth.

> This house hath been a fairy's dwelling-place
> As the immortals pure from head to feet
> Was she who stayed with us a little space,
> Then, as was meet,
> On her immortal journey went her ways.

> So wise was she—yet nothing but a flower;
> only a child—yet all the world to me;
> Against the stars what love hath any power
> Or was it she
> Went softly in her own appointed hour?

> The moon it was that called her, and she went;
> In Shiraz I had lived to live with her,
> Not knowing she was on errand bent—
> A traveller
> To sojourn for a night, then strike her tent.

> How sweet it was on many a summer's day
> On the green margin of the stream to lie
> With her and the wild rose, and nothing say;
> Little knew I
> That she was running like the stream away.

That was the sweet of life when, pure and wise,
In her dear bosom I drew my breath;
That was the truth of life—the rest is lies,
Folly and death,
Since toward another land she turned her eyes.

Blame her not, heart, because she left thee so;
The heaven of beauty called her to be queen;
Back to her hidden people must she go;
Behind the screen;
Nor when she will return doth Hafiz know. [1]

On the occasion of the death of his son, Hafiz wrote the following poems:

O heart, thou hast seen what that clever son
Has experienced within the dome of this multi-coloured
    vault;
In place of a silver slate in his hands
Fate hath placed a stone tablet on his head.

Little sleeper, the spring is here;
Tulip and rose are come again,
Only you in the earth remain,
Sleeping, dear;
Little sleeper, the spring is here;
I, like a cloud of April rain,
Am bending over your grave in vain,
Weeping, dear.

Little flower, the spring is here;
What if my tears were not in vain
What if they drew you up again,
Little flower. [2]

Most of Hafiz's poems were written in his later years, for he continually referred to himself as an old man and lamented the folly of so old a head being turned by such youthful passions. The names of some of his lovers occur

occasionally in the *Divan*—Selma, Ferrukh, for example—
but no stories connected with them have come down to us.
The roses have been forgotten. Only the nightingale is
remembered.

The following odes are a few samples of Hafiz's love
songs;

When thus I sit with roses in my breast,
Wine in my hand, and the beloved kind;
I ask no more—the world can take the rest.
Even the Sultan's self is, to my mind,
On such a lovely night as this,
Compared with me a veritable slave.

O love, if thou so cruel continuest to be,
Like other fool fanatics to the wilderness I'll flee,
And live on roots, religious-mad, up in the lovely moun-
tains;
My head turned with religion, the religion, love of thee.

Sweetheart, if you would hearken me,
I am a very wise old thing,
And it were wise for you to hear
My little Tatar, my cypress dear,
So wise this wisdom that I sing.

O love, the beauty of the moon is thine,
And on thy chin a little star doth shine
O how my soul desires the sight of thee,
And wishes to the windows of my eyes,
And to and fro about my body flies,
Half out of doors and half constrained within;
Ears all atremble for some word of thine,
Tongue tip-toe on the threshold of the lip,
And my full heart is like a stormy sea.

Last night, as half-asleep I dreaming lay,
Half-naked came she in her little shift,

With tilted glass, and verses on her lips;
Narcissus—eyes all shining for the fray,
Filled full of frolic to her wine-red lips,
Warm as a dewy rose, sudden she slips
Into my bed—just in her little shift.[3]

LeGalliene writes:

As with Omar Khayyam, the question of the literal or
symbolic meanings of the epicureanism of Hafiz has, of
course, been raised, and answered in the same way. Some
will have it that the wine of Hafiz was the wine of the
spirit, and the love he celebrates was the love of God.
There is a type of mind which always prefers to interpret
masterpieces after this fashion—abstract intelligences,
with a holy horror of flesh and blood, who love to de-
humanize literature and prove our great warm-hearted
classics cryptograms of fantastic philosophy or speculation. We need go no further than the Bible for an illustration. We open it at the greatest love-song in the world's
literature—that of Solomon—and we read:

My beloved spake, and said unto me, rise up, my love, my
fair one, and come away.
For, lo the winter is past, and rain is over and gone; the
flowers appear on earth; the time of the singing of the
birds is come, and the voice of the turtle is heard in the
land.
The fig-tree putteth forth her green figs, and the vines with
the tender grape give a good smell. Arise, my love, my
fair one, and come away.[4]

2

The traditional Persian regards the poems of Hafiz in
much the same light as the Orthodox Christians regard the
Song of Solomon. There are many Persians who respect
Hafiz as much as they honor a prophet. His book is

canonized and is found in every Persian home next to the
Qoran. The theologians who admire Hafiz today are different from their predecessors who were Hafiz's great
enemies and who tried to excommunicate him. On his
death, they attempted to prevent his being buried with religious rites, denouncing him as a heretic and a profligate.
Predicting this ugly situation, Hafiz had admonished his
enemies:

Withhold not thy attendance from the funeral of Hafiz; for,
though he is a chronic sinner, he would go to Heaven.[5]

Hafiz's belief in intellectual liberty was profound. His loyalty was to the truth, and he was a sworn enemy of hypocrisy. In an era when orthodoxy and fanaticism were dominant throughout the world, Hafiz labeled "the web of convention" as "the imbecility of those whom it entangles."

He shared with Homer contempt for unprincipled op-
portunists: "For I hold that man as hateful as the gates of
Hell who says one thing, while another in his heart lies
hidden."

When Mubarizud Din, who ruled Fars from 1353 to
1357, closed down all the taverns in the city of Shiraz and
forbade the sale of wine, Hafiz protested vigorously:

Though wine gives delight and the wind distils the perfume
of the rose,
Drink not wine to the strains of the harp, for the constable is
alert.
Hide the goblet in the sleeve of your prayer cloak,
For this era, like the eye of decanter pours forth blood.
Wash your holy cloak from the wine stain tears,
For it is the season of piety and the time of abstinence.

O will it be that they will reopen the doors of the taverns,
And will loosen the knots from our tangled affairs?

They have closed the doors of the wine-taverns; O God suffer not
That they should open the doors of the house of deceit and hypocrisy.
If they have closed them for the sake of the selfish zealot
Be of good cheer, for they will reopen them for God's sake.[6]

When Shah Shuja succeeded his father, Mubarizud Din, he relaxed his predecessor's oppressive restrictions and ordered the reopening of all the taverns.

The occasion was celebrated by Hafiz in the following verses:

At early dawn good tidings reached my ear from the heavenly voice:
It is the era of Shah Shuja: drink wine boldly
That time is gone when men of insight went apart
With a thousand words in their mind but their lips silent.
To the sound of the harp we will tell those stories
At the hearing of which the cauldron of our bosoms boiled.[7]

Another poem refers to those religious leaders who, after the death of Mubarizud Din, changed their tune and followed Shah Shuja in his liberal, anticlerical measures:

I swear by the glory and the honor and high position of Shah Shuja
That I have no quarrel with anyone on account of possession or position.
See how the one who in the past would not permit listening to music
Now goes dancing to the strains of the harp.[8]

In another poem, Hafiz attacks the religious leader of his time, Imadi Fagih, whose deceit had reached such lengths that his followers were spreading the rumor that he had taught his cat to recite prayers. The story was accounted by

Imadi's adherents as a miracle but by Hafiz as a charlatan's trick:

> The ascetic hath made display of his virtues and begun his
>   blandishments;
> He hath inaugurated his scheming with the mischievous
>   heavens.
> O graceful-moving partridge who walkest with the air of
>   confidence,
> Be not deceived because the cat of the ascetic hath said its
>   prayers.[9]

The scorn expressed by Hafiz for Shah Shuja's courtiers and religious leaders irritated the ruler who, as a mediocre poet, was jealous of Hafiz's fame and literary success. On one occasion Shah Shuja told Hafiz that his poems were mysterious, vague, and unclear. "No one motive," the Prince said, "inspires you; at one moment you are mystical, at another erotic and blasphemous; today serious and spiritual; tomorrow flippant, scornful, sarcastic and seductive." "True," replied Hafiz, "but in spite of all your criticism people from Fars to India know, admire and repeat my verses, while the poems of others never can pass beyond the gate of the city of Shiraz."

> The black-eyed beauties of Kashmir and the Turks of
>   Bukhara
> Sing and dance to the strains of Hafiz of Shiraz's verse.

> I have never seen any poetry sweeter than thine, O Hafiz,
> I swear by that Qoran which thou keepest in thy bosom.

Hafiz received respect and honor not only from the rulers of Shiraz. Many other princes sought Hafiz's friendship and the pleasure of his company. Sultan Ahmad, the ruler of Baghdad, himself a good poet, musician and painter, invited Hafiz to visit his court, but the latter refused:

The zephyr breeze of Musolla and the stream of Ruknabad
Do not permit me to travel or wander afield.[10]

However he composed verses in praise of Sultan Ahmad and sent them to him:

I praise God for the justice of the King Ahmad,
The son of Shaykh Uways, the son of Hassan Ilkhan;
A lord, the son of lord, a king of kingly descent,
Whom it were meet that I should call the soul of the world.[11]

Mahmud Shah of Deccan, in India, a liberal patron of poets, invited Hafiz to his country and sent him money for his journey. Hafiz divided a considerable portion of the money among his friends and students before he left Shiraz, and, on arriving at Lar on his way to the Persian Gulf, met with a needy friend to whom he gave the remainder. Two rich merchants who were traveling with Hafiz offered to pay all his expenses and accompany him to the court of Deccan. Hafiz traveled with them as far as Hurmuz, where a ship was waiting to take him to India, but just as he was embarking a tempest arose, frightening him so much that he abandoned his journey, returned to Shiraz, and sent the Sultan the following verses:

Not all the sum of earthly happiness,
Is worth the bowed head of a moment's pain,
And if I sell for wine my dervish dress,
Worth more than what I sell is what I gain;
Land where my Lady Love dwells, thou holdest me
Enchained; else Fars were but a barren soil,
Not worth the journey over land and sea, not worth the toil.

Down in the quarter where they sell red wine,
My holy carpet scarce would fetch a cup—
How brave a pledge of piety is mine,
Which is not worth a goblet foaming up.
Mine enemy heaped scorn on me and said;
Forth from the tavern gate; Why am I thrust
From off the threshhold? Is my fallen head not worth the
dust?

Fully easy seemed the sorrow of the sea
Lightened by hope of gain—hope flew too fast.
A hundred pearls were poor indemnity,
Not worth the blast.

The Sultan's crown, with priceless jewels set,
Encircles fear of death and constant dread;
It is a headdress much desired—and yet
Art sure 'tis worth the anger to the head?
'Twere best for thee to hide thy face from those
That long for thee; the conqueror's reward
Is never worth the army's long-drawn woes, worth fire and
sword.
Ah, seek the treasure of mind at rest
And store it in the treasury of Ease;
Not worth a loyal heart, a tranquil breast,
Were all the riches of thy lands and seas.
Ah, scorn, like Hafiz, the delights of earth,
Ask not one grain of favor from the base,
Two hundred sacks of jewels were not worth thy soul's dis-
grace.[12]

3

Considering the fine sensitivity and acute susceptibility
which irradiate Hafiz's poetry, it is remarkable how this
liberal and humane poet preserved the strength and serenity of his poetic imagination in the face of the bloody events
of his time. All Persia was in turmoil; Fars and Shiraz itself
did not escape this chaotic situation. Hafiz was eyewitness to

158 SUFISM

the assassination of kings, the devastation of cities, religious
feuds, fratricidal wars; quarrels between father and sons;
yet he seems to have regarded these events from a spiritual
eminence as if they were the little waves of an ocean; his
gaze was fixed rather on the unity of the ocean—on the
nature, the meaning and the purpose of the world.[13] His
hope, earnest prayers and purpose were to save man from
stupidity, strife, and self-destruction. Furthermore, he believed that God is with us at every turn. It is our pride,
indifference and ignorance which alienate us from the
truth and eventually destroy us.

For years our heart has been seeking Jamshid's glass of us,[14]
Begging from strangers what it already owned;
Seeking from lost men on the sea-shore
The pearl that is outside the confines of place and being.
I took my difficulty to the Magian priest yesterday,
So that, with his form discernment, he might solve the rid-
  dle.
I found him joyful and smiling, a goblet of wine in his hand,
And in that mirror he was beholding a hundred sights.
He whose heart, like a rosebud, hid the secret of Reality,
Noted the page of his mind from that copy.
I asked him: When did the sage give you this world-
  surveying mirror?
He answered: On that day when He created the blue vault
  of heaven.
This forlorn man—God is with him at every turn, but he
  has not seen him and, as from afar, cries: My God, my
  God;
That dear Comrade, said he, on whose account even the
  gibbet raised its head,
His crime consisted in manifesting secret things.
If the grace of the Holy Spirit vouchsafe help again,
Others too may do what the Christ did.
I said to him: What means the chain of the tresses of fair
  idols?
He replied: Hafiz is complaining of the length of Christmas
  night!

Again the times are out of joint; and again
For wine and the loved one's languid glance I am fain.
The wheel of fortune's sphere is a marvellous thing:
What next proud head to the lowly dust will it bring?
Or if my magian elder kindle the light,
Whose lantern, pray, will blaze aflame and be bright?
'Tis a famous tale, the deceitfulness of earth;
The night is pregnant; what will dawn bring to birth?
Tumult and bloody battle rage in plain:
Bring blood-red wine, and fill the goblet again.[15]

Hafiz believed that man was a rational animal whose mission was to build, help, harmonize and bring joy and happiness to his fellow men. But when he observed the events of his time, he saw his world plunging ever further into cruelty, conflict, madness, persecution, and oppression:

What ails the time? Is friendship then no more?
What has become of the old kindly days?
The world seemed once so safe and warm with friends, new
    men, new ways.
And living went with gust; existence wore
Brave feathers, and the jocund planet whirled gaily in
    heaven: now somewhat sadly ends that ancient world.

The water of life is muddied and bitter grown,
Clear as the immortal well it used to be;
That roses sicken and the breezes faint;
What aileth—me.
And when the roses bloom, they bloom alone,
No nightingales. I cannot understand—
What is the meaning of this mortal taint upon the land?
The world was once the birthplace of great Kings,
And there was music in it and many loves;
But now hath Venus burned her lute,
And slain her doves:
No one gets drunk any more and no one sings;
A melancholy world. Hafiz, it is
No world of thine.[16]

The ebbs and tides in the affairs of men saddened Hafiz's heart, but he always returned to sober thought and sought tranquility of heart and peace of mind in a world of confusion and chaos. Through the age of violent wars and dynastic feuds, he remained calm and dedicated to his principles.

Hafiz wrote with such brevity and beauty that since his time he has influenced the thoughts and the style of Persian writers.

> In the garden of the world, one rose
>   For me's enough;
> Many a fairer in that garden grows—
>   Mine's fair enough;
> Out in the meadow all the shade I ask
>   Falls from the cypress that I call my own;
> O canting Sufi, take us not to task—
>   Leave us alone;
> Weighty thy matter, but we find the stuff,
> Most learned doctor, in this portly flask
>   Heavy enough.
>
> After a well-spent life comes paradise,
> With palaces fair painted on the skies;
> We topers know a better heaven than this;
> The tavern, to our wayward thinking, is
>   Heaven enough.
>
> Upon the margin of the stream we sit
> And watch the world with a contented eye;
> The stream glides onward and ever, so it
> As surely passes by:
> Brief joy, long pain, is all the world can give;
> Pore on the stream and learn this lesson rough:
> If you the gain, we find the loss, to live
>   More than enough.
>
> To sit with the Beloved, who could more
> Ask of a world so very sad as this—
> Yea, even could a happier world give more?

Ah, drive me not, Beloved, from thy door
With harsh rebuff;
For knowest thou not thy doorstep is my home?
Nor send me to some distant realm of bliss—
No knowledge crave I of the world to come,
For never I of this old world that is
Can have enough.

Union with thee. I have no other thought;
In heaven's market I've no wish to buy:
Here I can see and handle what I have bought—
Not so the rainbow wares of yonder sky.[17]

Hafiz rarely indulged in flattery and was seldom guilty of exaggeration. He was a true master of eloquence, simplicity, frankness, honesty and decency. He hated dogmatism and hypocrisy. To men lost in the cobwebs of religious fanaticism, Hafiz was a heretic, and his poems were dismissed as the vaporings of a fool. Hafiz replied characteristically:

Heavens, do you think this is a time to choose
To give the good wine up?
Just at the very moment when the rose
In every garden blows.
How can I so unseasonably refuse
The spring's own cup?

Nay—call the minstrel. So with lyre and reed,
Roses and girls, and girls, and song and song,
I may at length my hoarded virtue use,
Ah, hoarded up too long.
For I am sick to death of all the schools,
And now at last, at last, that I am freed
Awhile from wisdom's fools,
Ah, full advantage of it will I take,
And my deep thirst for beauty and for wine
For once, at least, I will slake.

Talk to me not about the book of sin,

For friend, to tell the truth,
That is the book I would be written in—
It is so full of youth.

And, mark me, friend, when on the judgment day
The black book and the white
Are angel-opened there, in Allah's light,
For all to read what's writ;
Just watch how lonely the white book will be.
But the black book, wherein is writ my name—
My name, my shame, my fame,—
With busy readers all besieged you I see,
Yea, almost thumbed away—
So interesting it.

And as for this, my fatal love of wine,
Believe me, friend, it is no fault of mine—
'Tis fate, just fate; and surely you don't think
I fear a God that destined me to drink.
This life of Hafiz was the gift of God—
To God some day I'll give it back again;
Ah, have no fear, when Hafiz meets his God,
I know He will not call it lived in vain.[18]

Like all men of integrity and lofty ideas, Hafiz found
himself on more than one occasion a stranger among his
own people; at odds with some of his social peers and
superiors; admonished by hypocrites; attacked and accused
by loud and vicious hate-mongers, yet continuing his mission with resolution and steadfastness.

Preacher, it is all in vain you preach to me,
Nor business of anyone's but mine
Where I have sinned and what my end will be.

Two gallons of old wine, and two old friends
That know the world and well each other know,
A corner of the meadow, an old book,
A river's flow:

In such simplicity begins and ends
All that I ask of God—keep all the rest,
Luxurious world, but leave me this green nook;
I keep the best.

Unique are the times; in what rude hands,
Shiraz, is fallen thy beloved rose.
Yea, and these war-worn eyes of mine did see
Thy savage foe
Ride with my own true love to other lands.
So heaven repays its servants, well, red wine
There still remains to comfort thee and me,
Old friend of mine.

Here let us sit until the storm be passed;
In all the meadows scarce is left a flower,
So fierce a whirlwind smote our little town,
Wild to devour—
Patience, God will not suffer this to last:
The times are sick, and none knows who shall cure;
Best, Hafiz, in the cup thy griefs to drown
And so endure.

To a world cursed with war, burdened with overpopulation, sullied by pollution, and afflicted with the poverty and alienation of masses of people, Hafiz has a message of hope and consolation:

'Tis an unstable world: all fades and glides
And surely melts and vanishes away;
Even as the hollow wind we come and go,
Like the obliterating ebb and flow
Of wreck-encumbered shingle-shifting tides
Forgotten as the irridescent spray.

Saki (cup bearer), the servant of that man am I
Who kneels to nobody beneath the blue,
But firm in spirit, lets the world go by.
Come, fill the cup—I have stranger news for you,

How shall I utter what last night befell
Here in this reeking tavern unto me,
Drunk and adream and foolish with old wine.

"Hafiz forsake the world," I hear the angels sing;
Bride of a thousand bridegrooms hath she been,
This ancient painted woman; the same lie
Hath she told all, nor yet in anything
Hath she kept faith, expect not constancy,
Enamoured nightingale, from such a rose.

My heritage the tavern is—
Ah, such a pietist am I,
My abbot is the taverner—
Yea, such a pietist am I,
And every morning thus I pray:
Give us the red wine day by day,
God grant me too the sight of her.
Thus pray I to the taverner
Each morning at the break of day—
Such, such a pietist am I.

Beggar and King to me are one:
So very beautiful is she,
That any beggar who shall fling
Upon her doorstep in a dream
Shall surely seem to me a King.
Whatever else I do or seem,
Only one thought possesses me,
In mosque or tavern—it is she;
Living or dead, or damned,—it is she;
So very beautiful is she.[19]

Few Oriental poets have enjoyed as much praise from
Western savants as Hafiz. Ralph Waldo Emerson wrote:

Hafiz is the prince of the Persian poets; in his extraordinary gifts he adds to some of the attributes of Pindar,
Anacreon, Horace, and Burns the insight of a mystic, that

sometimes affords a deeper glance at nature than belongs to any of these bards. He accosts all topics with an easy audacity.

His was the fluent mind in which every thought and feeling came readily to the lips. "Loose the knots of the heart," he says, "We absorb elements enough, but have not leaves and lungs for healthy perspiration and growth. Hafiz has a great capacity for intellectual liberty, which is a certificate of profound thought. We accept the religions and politics into which we fall; and it is only a few spirits who are sufficient to see that the whole web of convention is the imbecility of those whom it entangles—that the mind suffers no religion and no empire but its own. It indicates this respect to absolute truth by the use it makes of the symbols that are most stable and revered, and therefore is always provoking the accusation of irreligion. Hypocrisy is the perpetual butt of Hafiz's arrows.[20]

Hafiz's frankness and courage surprises both Goethe and Emerson. In an age of fanaticism and religious bigotry, Hafiz tells his mistress that not the holy men, nor the monk, but the lover, has in his heart the spirit which makes the ascetic and the saint; and certainly not their cowls and mummeries, but her glances, can impart to him the fire and virtue needful for such self-denial. Wrong shall not be wrong to Hafiz for the name's sake. "A law or statute is to him what a fence is to a nimble schoolboy—a temptation for a jump." In answer to the religious leaders, Hafiz states: "We would do nothing but good; else would shame come to us on the day when the soul must lie hence;—and should they then deny us paradise, the Houris themselves would forsake that, and come out to us."[21]

The complete intellectual emancipation which Hafiz communicated to his readers profoundly impressed Emerson:

Nothing is too high, nothing too low, for his occasion. He
fears nothing, he stops for nothing. Love is a leveller, and
Allah becomes a groom, and heaven a closet, in his daring
hymns to his mistress or to his cupbearers. This boundless charter is the right of genius . . . We do not wish to
stew sugar on bottled spiders, or try to make mystical
divinity out of the songs of Solomon, much less out of the
erotic and bacchanalian songs of Hafiz. Hafiz himself is
determined to defy all such hypocritical interpretation,
and tears off his turban and throws it at the head of the
meddling dervish, and throws his glass after the turban.
But the love or the wine of Hafiz is not to be confounded
with vulgar debauch. Hafiz praises wine, roses, maidens,
boys, birds, mornings, and music, to give vent to his immense hilarity and sympathy with every form of beauty
and joy; and lays the emphasis on these to mark his scorn
of sanctimony and base prudence. These are the natural
topics and language of his wit and perception. But it is the
play of wit and the joy of song that he loves; and if you
mistake him for a low rioter, he turns short on you with
verses which express the poverty of sensual joys and to
ejaculate with equal fire the most unpalatable affirma-
tions of heroic sentiment and contempt for the world.[22]

There was no limit to Hafiz's respect for the freedom of
thought. His integrity, independence and individuality had
no bound. He claims that his ideas are manifestations of
human dignity, dedication, love and kindness. "They are
inspired by Heavenly inspirations, and their purpose is to
alert humankind against greed and lust for power, and
money and human exploitation. Man's mission was to help
and to avoid hurting his fellow men!"[23]

Where is the pious doer? and I the estray'd one, where?
Behold how far the distance, from his safe home to here.
Dark is the stony desert, trackless and vast and dim,
Where is hope's guiding lantern? Where is faith's star so
    fair?

My heart fled from cloister, and chant of monkish hymn,
What can avail me—sainthood, fasting and punctual
  prayer?

What is the truth shall light me to heaven's strait thoroughfare?
Whither, O heart, thou hastest? Arrest thee, and beware.

See what a love adventure is thine unending quest.
Fraught with what deadly danger. Set with what unseen
  snare.
Say not, a friend to Hafiz, "quiet thee now and rest."
Calm and content, what are they? Patience and peace, O
  where?[24]

. . . . .
The rose has flushed red, the bud has burst,
And drunk with joy is the nightingale—
Hail Sufis, lovers of wine, all hail.
For wine is proclaimed to a world athirst.

Like a rock your repentance seemed to you;
Behold the marvel, of what avail
Was your rock, for a goblet has cleft it in two.

Bring wine for the King and the slave at the gate.
Alike for all is the banquet spread,
And drunk and sober are warmed and fed.

When the feast is done and the night grows late,
And the second door of the tavern gapes wide,
The low and the mighty must bow the head
'Neath the archway of Life, to meet what . . . outside?[25]

Every song of Hafiz shows how little importance he attached to worldly success. He asserts the dignity of man and
emphasizes service and decency as the greatest human virtues. To a rich man returning from a pilgrimage to Mecca,
he says: "Boast not rashly of thy fortune, Thou hast visited
the temple; but I have seen the Lord of the temple."

Oft have I said, I say it once more—
I, a wanderer, do not stray from myself.
I am a kind of parrot; the mirror is holden to me;
What the master of eternity says, I stammering say again.

Ah, Sufi, can you dream I will give up
A love like this—for pious platitude,
Or cease to crush the grape into the cup.
I, Sufi, may be wrong, you may be right—
Hafiz must tread his self-appointed way
And on her red lips find his heavenly food.
If you must talk, O talk some other day—
But not to-night.

Beloved, blame him not if, for relief,
The sanctuary of his ruined heart,
Nursing the precious treasure of his grief,
Unto the kindly tavern Hafiz brings;
Nor talk of shame to Hafiz—for his part,
Nowise ashamed is Hafiz of his shame;
That which the world accounts a spotless name
Hafiz, indeed, would be ashamed to bear.
Wine-bibber call him, and adulterer.
Go on. What else, he will not say thee nay.

Is Shiraz then so innocent a place
That none but Hafiz ever goes astray
After the wine-cup and a pretty face?
Summon the censor, he who takes such care
Of us poor fools—he's always running after
Women and wine—the very same as we;
Be sure he also loves good wine and laughter.
Nay, Zahid, go thy ways, let Hafiz be.
To-night the never-ending fast is done,
And the great feast comes in with minstrelsy:
Here shall we sit, until the rising sun
Glitters on rose and jasmine—I and she.[26]
. . . . .
Surely you must not ask of me the cause
Why mortal beauty breaks immortal laws;

No reason can I give, save this alone
That beauty's self for beauty's sins alone:
Reason enough, though reasonless it seems—
The lovely rainbow reason of our dreams.

Love is a sea that hath not any shore,
And help upon that shoreless sea is none;
Who sails it sets his eyes on land no more;
Yet gladly am I on that voyage gone—
For ah, how good it is to sail that sea.
What though the longest trip at last be o'er.
What though the proudest vessel must go down,
My love is on the same big ship with me,
And when she drowns, I drown.

Talk not of reason to a man in love,
Nor pit thy arguments against good wine;
Love has a wisdom, wisdom cannot prove—
Reason knows nothing of the things divine.

Love is a church where all religions meet;
Islam, or Christ, or tavern, it is one;
The face of every system is the sun—
O sun that shines in the Beloved's street.

Where love is there is no need of convent hell,
And holy living needs no holy frocks;
Time ticks not to your monastery clocks;
Where goodness is there God must be as well.[27]

4

Hafiz's mystical ideas had a great influence on Goethe.
After the completion of the *Sonnet Cycle* and the *Wahlverw*
and *Tschaften*, Goethe's fountain of inspiration went almost
dry. For five years he could not produce any poetic work of
significance. He sought some new experience mighty
enough to "again quicken his creative force—something
which would assail the whole inner man, spirit and heart."

The longed-for rejuvenation of his giant brain came from an unknown source—Hafiz.

In his youth Goethe had shown great interest in the Islamic tradition and ideas. He had studied the Qoran carefully and had called Muhammad a religious genius. But his enthusiasm and inclinations waned when his Italian experiences made Greek antiquity his highest norm.[28]

It was late in the summer of 1814 that Goethe came across the first German translation of Hafiz's odes, which had been freely translated by Joseph von Hammer-Purgstall of Vienna. A new world was opened to him. "I had to respond with productivity," wrote Goethe, "because otherwise I could have not stood up to this imposing figure."[29] The unexpected inspiration produced a new epoch of rich productivity for the aging man. How near were Hafiz's ideas to Goethe's mature mind? Very close:

> An old man had made these poems; they showed the dark colours of a late love and the quenched glow of a joy in life which rested upon the tranquil ground of mature wisdom and free piety. In addition to sharing common spiritual and moral attitudes, both poets experienced a common historical fate. While kingdoms collapsed about him and usurpers sprang up, Hafiz imperturbably sang of nightingales and roses, of wine and love. This poetry was like a mirror which reflected to Goethe the image of his own situation in the transfiguring illumination of a great past. From the inspiring present and its crippling unrest Goethe could take refuge in the spiritual reality of this remote art.[30]

Before Goethe was an example of a great poet who had raised himself above the chaotic events of his time into the realm of great spiritual values. He followed Hafiz's example:

North and West and South are breaking,
Thrones are bursting, kingdoms shaking:
Flee, then, to the essential East,
Where on Patriarch's air you'll feast.
There to love and drink and sing,
Drawing youth from Khizr's spring.

Pure and righteous there I'll trace
To its source the human race,
Prime of nations, when to each
Heavenly truth in earthly speech
Still by God himself was given,
Human brains not racked and riven.

When they honored ancestors,
To strange doctrine closed their doors.
Youthful bounds shall be my pride,
My thought narrow, my faith wide.
And all I'll find the token word
Dear because a spoken word.

Mix with goatherds in dry places,
Seek refreshment in oases
When with caravans I fare,
Coffee shawls, and mask my ware,
Every road and path explore,
Desert, cities, and seashore.

Holy Hafiz, you in all
Baths and taverns I'll recall,
When the loved one lifts her veil,
Ambergris her locks exhale.
More: the poet's love song must
Melt the houris, move their lust.

Now should you begrudge him this,
Even long to spoil such bliss,
Poet's words, I'd have you know,
Round the gate of Eden flow,
Gently knocking without rest,
Everlasting life their quest.[31]

Goethe, in his *West-Eastern Divan,* like Hafiz, escapes from
the painful world of conflict to the realm of love and hope.
He admits that his knowledge of Hafiz and his philosophy
enabled him to rejuvenate his life.

The poem at the beginning of Goethe's *Divan* is called
"Hegira," after the Prophet Mohammad's flight from
Mecca to Medina. Goethe's flight was "no flight into exile
and frustrations: a man called to greatness sought conditions which would permit him to inaugurate his work."[32]
His escape from the paralyzing present was also a hegira.
Goethe always sought truth; therefore it should not sur-
prise anybody that the poet of the West, the follower of
Plato and Homer, was ready and pleased to look for new
ideas in the East, "the land of faith and of revelations,
prophecies, and promises." Goethe found the philosophy of
the Persian poet acceptable because of its deep and basic
earnestness: Hafiz's odes and ideas differed from character-
less and actionless yearning.

> To God belongs the Orient.
> To God belongs the Occident.
> Northern lands and southern lands
> Rest in quiet of his hands.

> He who is the only just one
> Wills justice for everyone.
> Of his hundred names, be then
> This most highly praised. Amen.

> By error I must entangled be:
> Yet thou canst disentangle me.
> In what I invent, in what I act
> Show my way thou dost direct.

> In breathing air, there are two kinds of graces:
> Air one takes in, and air that one releases:
> That one is effort, this other one revives;

So wonderful the mixing of our lives.
Thank God then, thou each time he presses thee,
And thank him when he next releases thee.[33]

The above verses are based on a story of the *Gulistan* of Sadi of Shiraz which the German Orientalist, Adam Olearius, had translated into German. Goethe found in this story a simple piety which expressed his own faith.[34]

Goethe's *Divan* is rich in gnomic verse; indeed, reflective, mystic poetry dominates it. This was appropriate to the poet's years of reflection. He combined thought and perception, mystic ideas and reality.

This creative synthesis is magnificently evident in his poem ".The Spiritual Yearning." The poem speaks of the ideas so often expressed in Hafiz's odes: a yearning of the ego for exaltation by surrender, by self-effacement, by seeking entity with the beloved and the discovery of true freedom:

> Tell it only to the wise,
> For the crowd at once will jeer:
> That which is alive I praise,
> That which longs for death by fire.

> Cooled by passionate love at night,
> Procreated, procreating,
> You have known the alien feeling
> In the calm of candle light;

> Gloom-embraced will lie no more,
> By the flickering shades obscured,
> But are seized by new desire,
> To a higher union lured.

> Then no distance holds you fast;
> Winged, enchanted, on you fly,

Light your longing, and at last,
Moth you meet the flame and die.

Never prompted to that quest:
Die and dare rebirth.
You remain a dreary guest
On our gloomy earth.[35]

Goethe adopted from the following ode of Hafiz the
motif of the first stanza—the simile of the soul burning like
a tapèr in the fire of love—and the metaphor of the moth.
"It is in the surrender of the ego, in its union with "thou,"
that man gains experience of the highest rapture vouchsafed him this life; and at the same time he achieves an
enhancement of his own individuality which may be attained in no other way. The supreme moment of the rapture of love symbolizes this experience which is valid for all
stages and all realms of our being. The soul, the moth, seeks
redemption from the strait limits of its individual existence;
it desires to dissolve in union with something infinite."[36]

That, that is not the flame of love's true fire
Which makes the torchlight shadows dance in rings,
But where the radiance draws the moth's desire
And sends him forth with scorched and drooping wings.
The heart of one who dwells retired shall break,
Remembering a black mole and a red cheek,
And his life ebb, sapped at its secret springs.

Yet since the earliest time that man has sought
To comb the locks of speech, his goodly bride,
Not one, like Hafiz, from the face of thought
Has torn the veil of ignorance aside.[37]

Goethe studied Hafiz's odes at a time when he was not
happy with his world and what he saw in it. The powerful
language of Hafiz's odes also displayed the maturity, the

intellectual nobility and the universalism of an old and noble culture. "The invigorating incitement derived from the encounter with Hafiz was supplemented and enhanced by the mightily burgeoning feeling of a new youth." This produced the *Divan*, which "is not merely a book of lyric wisdom, it is also a compendium of late, mature love poetry." In his poems of wisdom based on Hafiz's *Divan*, Goethe, the aging master, is in complete control of his art, in complete control also of the inward life which finds expression in these poems. A social spirit is here everywhere apparent. Emotions and thoughts are uttered in these poems in a relaxed, frequently conversational style:[38]

Thou mayst choose a thousand forms to hide thee,
Yet, all beloved, I shall know thee there;
Thou mayst take enchanted veils to shroud thee,
Yet, thou all present, I shall feel thee near.

In the pure springing of the tall young cypress,
All-stateliest, I know thee well the while,
In the pure lakelet's limpid, laughing ripple,
Thou all-beguiler, I behold thy smile.

And when the fountain lifts her jet and opens,
All-playfullest, I gaze upon thy glee,
And when the cloud-forms change their changing fashion,
All-myriad-natured, I am sure of thee.

Gay in the meadow's flower-embroidered raiment,
All-starry brightness, I can see thy face;
Where the light-handed ivy climbs and clusters,
All-clamberer, I catch thy eager grace.

When the new morning flames upon the mountains,
All-gladdener, gladly I welcome thee,
And when the pure sky arches out above us,
All-heart enlarger, I know it breathes of thee.

If aught I learn by outward sense or inward,
All-learned teacher, I learn it all through thee,
And when I name the hundred names of Allah,
There echoes with each one a name for thee.[39]

As on the day that brought thee to this earth
The sun stood in conjunction with the stars,
So art thou fashioned by the heavenly laws
That mark thy ways and walk with thee from birth.

Thus art thou stamped: thyself thou canst not flee.
Thus spake the sibyls, thus the prophets spake.
Not vastly time nor any power can break
The living form that grows eternally.[40]

It comes at last. From heaven it falls, down-dancing,
Whither from ancient chaos up it flew;
Around it floats, now near, and then departing.
It fans the brow and breast the spring-day through:

Rousing vague longings for the Fair and True,
While most hearts fade away, unfixed, alone,
The noblest is devoted to the one.[41]

No longer on sheets of silk
Symmetrical rhymes I paint,
No longer from them
In golden Arabesques;
Imprinted on mobile dust
They are swept by the wind, but their
Power endures,
As far as the center of Earth,
Riveted, bound to the soil.
And the wanderer will come,
The lover, if he enters
This place, all his limbs
Will feel the thrill.
"Here, before me, the lover loved.
Was it Mejnun, the tender?
Farhad, the strong? was it Djemil, the obstinate?

Or one of a thousand other
Happy, unhappy men?
He loved, I love as he loved.[42]

At midnight, I was sleeping in my breast
My fond heart lay awake, as though it were day;
Day broke: as though by falling night oppressed
I thought: what's day to me, bring what it may?

Since she was lacking; all my toil and strife
For her alone patiently I'd withstood
Throughout the hot noon hours. What quickening life
In the cool evening, blessed it was, and good.

The sun went down; and hand to dear hand wedded
We took our leave of him, watched the last ray burn,
And the eye said, eye to clear eye threaded:
But hope, and from the East he will return.[43]

Hafiz warns his readers against vanity and its disastrous
consequences in the following odes:

O let not vanity and avarice tempt thy wild desires
To toil for fame and wealth in fortune's glittering mine.
Small is the pittance mortal man requires,
And trifling labor makes that pittance thine.

> House of vanity is built on sand,
> And life's foundations rest on air,
> Then come, give wine into my hand
> That we may make an end of care.

> Let me be slave to that man's will
> Who 'neath high heaven's turquoise bowl
> Hath won and winneth freedom still
> From all vanities and entanglement of soul;
> Save that the mind entangled be
> With her whose radiant loveliness
> Provoking love and loyalty
> Relieves the mind of all distress.

Be pleased with what the fates bestow,
Nor let thy brow be furrowed thus;
The gate to freedom here below
Stands not ajar to such as us.

Look not to find fidelity
Within a world as weakly stayed;
This ancient crone, are flouting thee,
A thousand bridegrooms had betrayed.[44]

Trust not in fortune, vain deluded charm.
Whom wise men shun and only vain fools adore.
Oft, while she smiles, fate sounds the dread alarm,
Round flies her wheel; you sink to rise no more.

Ye rich and great, why rear those vain princely domes?
Those heavens-aspiring towers why proudly raise?
Lo, whilst triumphant all around you blooms,
Death's awful angel numbers out your days.

But to the fair no longer be a slave;
Drink, Hafiz, revel, all your cares unbend,
And boldly scorn the vain dissembling knave
Who makes religion every vice defend.[45]

   Goethe, being inspired by Hafiz, appropriates the spirit
of the great master and freely and masterfully elaborates on
Hafiz's philosophy in the following poem:

> I have set my heart upon nothing you see;
> Hurrah.
> And so the world goes well with me.
> Hurrah.
> And who has a mind to be fellow of mine.
> Why, let him take hold and help me twine
> A wreath for the rosy nine.
>
> I set my heart at first upon wealth;
> Hurrah.

And bartered away my peace and health;
But ah,

The slippery change went about like air;
And when I had clutched me a handful here,
Away it went there.
I set my heart upon travels grand,
Hurrah,
And spurned our plain old fatherland;
But ah,
Naught seemed to be just the thing it should,
Most comfortless beds and indifferent fools,
    My taste misunderstood.
I set my heart upon sounding fame;
Hurrah,
And lo, I am eclipsed by some upstart's name;
And, ah,
When in public life I loomed quite high,
The folks that passed me would look away;
Their worst friend was I.
And then I set my heart upon war.
Hurrah.
We gained some battles with éclat.
Hurrah.
We troubled the foe with sword and flame—
And some of our friends fared quite the same.
I lost a leg for fame.
Now I've set my heart upon nothing, you see;
Hurrah.
And the whole wide world belongs to me.
Hurrah.
The feast begins to run low, no doubt;
But at the old spring we'll have one good bout.
Come, drink the waters out.[46]

Goethe believes that the general characteristic of Hafiz's
poetry is the dominance of higher guidance. In those verses
one witnesses the ripe intellectuality of an epoch which usually expresses itself as wit and irony.

Goethe's *Divan,* based and named after Hafiz's *Divan,* appeared in 1819 in his seventieth year. "An old man to whom the vigor of his prime was momentarily restored wrote the *Divan.* A man tired of life but not discouraged, a sagacious man, whose deeper insight has not made him a skeptic, speaks in it. Unexpectedly life is restored to him and grants him a last intensification. Once more love and the sense of full existence raise him to a state in which devout wisdom and the fire of passion interpenetrate and achieve unique fullness and wholesomeness."[47]

He calls this part of his life a merger of the past with present exaltation. Spirit was the clear force of cosmic comprehension, not practical rationality, nor yet metaphysical speculation. Hafiz gave Goethe a spirit of detachment and sovereign freedom. He admired in Hafiz's poetry that supreme soaring of the soul "where the tension between yearning and wise resignation is resolved in a unification of opposites—something man can achieve only in rare moments of life."

Goethe describes Hafiz: " . . . contented in straitness, joyous and wise, taking his own portion of the world's abundance, looking from afar into the secrets of the Godhead, but on the other hand rejecting alike religious practice and sensual pleasure. Intense delight in life keeps the spirit from becoming heavy and gloomy."[48]

To Goethe, Hafiz's love poems enjoyed ever present rationality, always sure of itself, a perfection which was "the symbolic expression of the fact that here the marriage of form-fashioning consciousness and infinite passion has been consummated."

Hafiz, according to Goethe, produced a work of singular abundance and sublimity. "Wisdom and piety, the happiness of the senses and of the heart, love and beauty, lordly play of spirit and reverent earnestness are in it combined into an image of perfection."[49]

After the discovery of Hafiz, Goethe appeals to the Persian poet to lead him through the dangerous track of life:

> Dangerous track, through rock and scree:
> Hafiz, there you'll comfort me
> When the guide, enchanted, tells
> On the mule's back, your ghazels,
> Sings them for the star to hear,
> Robber bands to quail with fear.[50]

> Who never ate his bread with tears,
> Who never through the long night hours
> Sat weeping on his bed of fears
> He knows you not, you heavenly powers.

> Into our life you lead us in,
> The wretch's guilt you bring to birth,
> Then bring affliction down on sin,
> For all guilt takes revenge on Earth.

> Who gives himself to loveliness,
> Ah, he is soon alone;
> Each lives, each loves, and comfortless
> Leaves him to pine alone.

> Yes, leave me to my bane,
> And if but once I can
> Make solitude my own,
> Then I am not alone.[51]

5

As long as there is life and love in the Persian-speaking world, "as long as life will love itself and not tire of its sweet sorrow nor turn wearily from itself," Hafiz is alive, and, according to his own prophecy, the black-eyed beauties of Kashmir and the Turks of Bukhara sing and dance to the strains of Hafiz of Shiraz's verse.

Shibli Nemani believes that Hafiz exerted a mighty influence on world culture through his universal philoso-

phy, humanistic attitude, beautiful odes, and his unique
personality. He attracts universal attention and evokes
universal fascination by his expression of world brotherhood:

> Brothers, attend
> How ye shall spend
> This fleeting treasure
> Of days that pass
> Fill ye your measure
> With present pleasure,
> The deep sweet gloss,
> And love and leisure
> And sunny grass.
>
> Let the pious thunder
> Of heaven and hell
> He drinks as well;
> Let the proud man rear
> His lofty towers:
> Have ye no fear,
> The little flowers
> That grow under
> Shall last as long
> Or a little song.
>
> Nor our most high Lord
> The Sultan's sword
> Can more command,
> When he comes to die,
> Than you and I
> Of simple birth
> Can ask of earth
> A little land
> In which to die.
>
> And even now,
> Who would ask
> Than just to bask

The blue sky under:
A little grass,
Wine in the glass,
One's liberty
And love and wonder:
This Hafiz, is felicity.[52]

Beauty alone will not account for her;
No single attribute her charm explain;
Though each be named, beyond it glimmers she,
Strangely distinct, mysteriously fair:
Hers this, this hers, and this—yet she remains.
Wonderful are her locks—she is not there;
Her body a spirit is—it is not she;
Her waist the compass of a silken thread;
Her mouth a ruby—but it is not she:
Say all of her, yet hast thou nothing said.
Surely the beauty of houri or of Fay
A fashion of beauty is—but to my eye
Her way of beauty is beauty's only way.[53]

Therefore, wise heart, it were safer to abide
In solitude, and to the cypress cling
That spreads its skirts upon the river side—
And lo! The east wind brings us news of spring.[54]

Abu Ishaq,[55] again, I thought upon,
So lately was he the hero of Shiraz here;
But where today is Abu Ishaq gone?
The ups and downs of this unstable sphere!
The city's laws his turquoise seals no more.
Hafiz, it was only yesterday we heard
That strutting partridge noise his vanished state;
Blind, like us all, he was not, foolish bird,
Poised in the clouds the falcon of his fate—
Alas! for his deserted palace door!

Comfort thee, heart—this much at least is true:
Nothing forever lasts, and this thy pain,
Even as thy joy is gone will leave thee too;
Nothing remains
Of all this grief that is so near and new.

Though as the wayside dust to her art thou,
Cherish not envy of thy rival's state:
It will some day be with him as with thee now;
None to be great
More than a moment the high Gods allow.

My friend! Ah yes: fill all the sky with heroes
Against me be heaven and earth and hell allied,
Darken the earth with armies, thick as the rose—
I care not if my Friend is on my side.

Draw off thy woolen coat that Sufi lie,
And draw the red wine in; and straightway spend
Such gold and silver as thou hast laid by
Upon some little silver-bosomed friend![56]

Unquiet are the times; in what rude hands,
Shiraz is fallen thy beloved rose!
Yea! and these war-worn eyes of mine did see thy savage
    heroes
Ride with my own true love to other lands.
So heaven repays its servants! Well, red wine
There still remains to comfort thee and me,
Old friend of mine.

Patience! God will not suffer this to last;
The times are sick and none knows who shall cure;
Best, Hafiz, in the cup thy griefs to drown,
And so endure.[57]

Sir Gore Ouseley, who visited Iran at the beginning of the
nineteenth century, describes Hafiz in the following words:
"His style is clear, unaffected and harmonious, displaying

at the same time great learning, matured science, and intimate knowledge of the hidden as well as the apparent nature of things; but above all a certain fascination of expression unequalled by any other poet."[58]
Gertrude L. Bell, an Orientalist who translated many of Hafiz's odes into English at the end of the nineteenth century, gives a critical, objective and masterful evaluation of Hafiz and his literary work:

> To Hafiz ... modern instances have no value; contemporary history is too small an episode to occupy his thoughts. During his lifetime the city which he loved, perhaps as dearly as Dante loved Florence, was besieged and taken five or six times; it changed hands even more often. It was drenched with blood by one conqueror, filled with revelry by a second, and subjected to the hard rule of asceticism by a third. One after another Hafiz saw Kings and Princes rise into power and vanish 'like snow upon the desert's dusty face.' Pitiful tragedies, great rejoicings, the fall of kingdoms and the clash of battle—all these he must have seen and heard. But what echo of them is in his poems? Almost none.
> But some of us will feel that the apparent indifference of Hafiz lends to his philosophy a quality which that of Dante did not possess.
> The Italian is bound down within the limits of his philosophy, his theory of the universe is essentially of his own age, and what to him was so acutely real is to many of us merely a beautiful or a terrible image. The picture that Hafiz draws represents a wider landscape, though the immediate foreground may not be so distinct. It is as if his mental eye, endowed with wonderful acuteness of vision, had penetrated into those provinces of thought which we of a later age were destined to inhabit. We can forgive him for leaving to us so indistinct a representation of his own time, and of the life of the individual in it, when we find him formulating ideas as profound as the warning that there is no musician to whose music both the drunk and the sober can dance.[59]

The best explanation of Hafiz's ideas and philosophy as expressed by Gertrude Bell are found in his poems:

Bring wine for the King and the slave at the gate!
Alike for all is the banquet spread,
And drunk and sober are warmed and fed.
When the feast is done and the night grows late,
And the second door of the tavern gapes wide,
The low and the mighty must bow the head
'Neath the archway of Life, to meet what . . . outside?
Except thy road through affliction pass,
None may reach the halting-station of mirth;
God's treaty: Am I not Lord of the earth?
Man sealed with a sigh: Ah yes, alas!
Nor with is nor is not let thy mind contend;
Rest assured all perfection of mortal birth
In the great is not at the last shall end.
For Solomon's pomp, and the steeds of the wind,
And the speech of birds down the wind have fled,
And be that was lord of them all is dead;
Of his pomp nothing remains behind.

The King's crown, with priceless jewels set,
Encircled fear of death and constant dread;
It is a headdress much desired—and yet
Art sure 'tis worth the danger to the head?

This ten-day smile of heaven swift passes like a tale told!
Be gracious while thou mayest, brook not procrastination
When comes the hour of sadness, turn thou to wine and
    gladness;
Qarun[60] of beggars maketh wine's chemic transmutation.

My bosom graced with each gay flower,
I grasp the bowl, my nymph in glee;
The monarch of the world that hour,
Is but a slave compared to me.

Then let no moments steal away,
Without thy mistress and thy wine;

The spring flowers blossom to decay,
And youth but glows to our decline.[61]

No wonder then, if in heaven to the words of Hafiz
The song of Venus entices to dance Messiah himself.

Thy passion dwells in my whole being, thy love inhabits my
   heart;
Entered my body with my mother's milk, and will leave it
   with my life.
What care if sober or drunk, every man is seeking the
   Friend;
What care if in mosque or church, each place is the house of
   love.

Erase everything you have copied into your book of life, if
   you would be my fellow man,
For the lesson of love is not to be found in books.
So full is my soul's horizon of the beloved
All thought of self has gone from my mind.

Love's physician has the healing breath of Jesus Himself
   and is full of compassion;
But if He find no pain in you, how will He administer a
   remedy?
I humbly bow to the Lord of the age
Who has the outward show of lordship and the inner spirit
   of a dervish.

Between the lover and the beloved there must be no veil;
Thou thyself art thy own veil, Hafiz—get out of the way.

   Sometimes in the verses of Hafiz one notices the voice of
skepticism and resignation. He laments that most of life's
abundance has been already taken from him; then he asks
himself what is left to make life rewarding? His answer is:
"Ideas and love."

   A grievous folly shames my sixtieth year—

My white head is in love with a green maid;
I kept my heart a secret, but at last I am betrayed.
Like a mere child I walked into the snare;
My foolish heart followed my foolish eyes;
And yet, when I was young—in ages past—I was so wise.
Ah! It was always so with us who sing!
Children of fancy, we are in the power
Of any dream, and at the bidding we of a mere flower;
Yet Hafiz, though full many a foolish thing
Ensnared thy heart with wonder, never thou
Wert wont imagination's slave to be
As thou art now.[62]

Forget not, O my heart, thine ancient friends:
The sweet old faithful faces of the dead,
Old meetings and old partings—all that ends;
So loved, so vivid, and so vanished:
Forget not, O my heart, thine ancient friends
The times are faithless, but remember thou
Those that have loved thee, though they love no more;
Thou unto them art dim and distant now;
Still love them for the love they gave before—
The times are faithless, but remember thou.

'Twere a sad world without a lover's voice;
Their lamentations are as sweet as birds;
And, when the little creatures do rejoice,
What pretty words
The dictionary yields up to their choice;
O love, continue to sustain the pride of this poor fly that
    dares to worship thee;
Mere hopeless love hath him so magnified, that seemed he
A bird of paradise all rainbow-dyed.

Hafiz, take heart; love is a grievous lord;
But this will always be the lover's creed,
Under the very shadow of lover's sword;
No gentle deed,
And no sweet action fails of its reward.
Well, Hafiz, Life's a riddle—give it up
There is no answer to it but this cup.[63]

Hafiz, methinks, at last thou growest old:
Loving and drinking were so easy once,
A mighty wencher wert thou in thy day,
But now at both thou art a perfect dunce;
Now is thy soul aweary, thy warm blood cold,
And all thy spirit wasted quite away.[64]

1. Richard LeGallienne, *Odes from the Divan of Hafiz*, Duckworth and Co. Ltd., London, 1905.
2. *Ibid.*, pp. 101, 185.
3. *Ibid.*, pp. 64–66.
4. *Ibid.*, p. 26.
5. Hafiz, *Divan*, Teheran Press, 1942, p. 52.
6. Edward G. Browne, *A History of Persian Literature*, vol. III, Cambridge University Press, Cambridge, 1920, p. 277.
7. *Ibid.*, p. 279.
8. Translated by the authors.
9. *Ibid.*
10. Browne, *op. cit.*, vol. III, p. 280–85.
11. *Ibid.*, p. 284.
12. Hafiz, *Divan*, translated by Gertrude Bell, p. 160.
13. Riza Zadah Shfaq, *Tarikh i Adabiyat*, Teheran, 1952, pp. 332–36.
14. Jam i-Jam was a crystal ball belonging to the mythical King Jamshid, through which he could see everything and foretell the future.
15. Hafiz, translated by Gertrude Bell, p. 162.
16. Hafiz, translated by Richard LeGallienne, London, Duckworth & Co., 1905 p. 97.
17. *Ibid.*, pp. 122–23.
18. *Ibid.*, p. 142.
19. Le Gallienne; *op. cit.*, pp. 23–31.
20. *The Works of Ralph Waldo Emerson*, Tudor Publishing Co., New York, 1920, pp. 416–21.
21. *Ibid.*
22. *Ibid.*, pp. 416–21.
23. Ghani, Gassem; Introduction to the Divan of Hafiz, Teheran, 1935, p. 68.
24. Hafiz, *Divan*, translated by Elizabeth Bridges, p. 84.
25. Hafiz, *Divan*, translated by Gertrude Bell, p. 68.
26. Hafiz, *Divan*, translated by Richard LeGallienne, p. 45.
27. *Ibid.*, p. 67.
28. Karl Vietor, *Goethe the Poet*, Harvard University Press, Cambridge, 1949, pp. 221–24.
29. *Ibid.*, p. 221.
30. *Ibid.*
31. Stephen Spender, *Great Writings of Goethe*, New York Mentor Books, 1958, p. 262.
32. *Ibid.*, p. 263.
33. *Ibid.*, p. 265.
34. Goethe borrows this idea from Sadi, the famous poet of Shiraz. Sadi's statement: "Laudation to the God of majesty and glory. Obedience to him is a cause of approach and gratitude in increase of benefits. Every inhalation of the breath prolongs life and every expiration of it gladdens our nature; wherefore

every breath confers two benefits and for every benefit gratitude is due. Whose hand and tongue is capable to fulfill the obligations of thanks to Him?"

35. Goethe, translated by Michael Hamburger, p. 266.
36. *Ibid.*
37. Hafiz, *Divan*, translated by Gertrude Bell.
38. Vietor, *Goethe the Poet, op. cit.*, pp. 222–25.
39. Thomas Mann, *The Permanent Goethe* (Zuleika), Dial Press, New York, 1929, translated by F. Melian Stawell, p. 652.
40. *Ibid.*, p. 650.
41. *Ibid.*, translated by James F. Clarke, p. 651.
42. Spender, *op. cit.*
43. *Ibid.*
44. Hafiz, *Divan*, translated by Arthur J. Arberry, p. 89.
45. *Ibid.*, translated by J. Richardson, p. 88.
46. Johann Goethe, *Vanitas*, The International Library of Famous Literature, vol. XVI, p. 7580, London, 1900.
47. Vietor, *op. cit.*, p. 230.
48. *Ibid.*
49. *Ibid*, p. 230.
50. Spender, *op. cit.*, p. 263.
51. *Ibid.*
52. Le Gallienne, Richard, *Odes from Divan of Hafiz*, op. cit. pp. 6–7.
53. *Ibid.*, p. 76.
54. *Ibid.*, p. 83.
55. Abu Ishaq was the lord and powerful governor of Shiraz. He was defeated and murdered in one of the upheavals of Fars.
56. *Ibid.*, p. 121.
57. *Ibid.*, p. 164.
58. Sir Gore Ouseley; *Biographical Notices of Persian Poets*, London, 1826, p. 23.
59. Gertrude L. Bell, *Poems from the Divan of Hafiz*, London, 1897, pp. 71–72.
60. Qarun in the Persian mythology is supposed to be the richest man in the world.
61. A. J. Arberry, *Classical Persian Literature*, the Macmillan Company, New York, 1958, pp. 343–44.
62. Le Gallienne, *op. cit.*, pp. 103–104.
63. *Ibid.*, p. 157.
64. *Ibid.*, p. 139.

8

Nizami Ganjai, the Love of Sufism

How many tales does slander frame,
And rumour whisper 'gainst my fame;
With malice both combine:
Because I wish to pass my days
Despising what each snarler says,
With friendship, love, and wine.

Nizami Ganjai (A.D. 1141–1205) is one of the great poets whose pathetic love songs and mystical lyrics illustrate the grace and beauty of the Persian spirit and language. Sadi, the famous Iranian savant and poet, writes in praise of him: "Gone is Nizami, our priceless pearl of wisdom, which heaven, in its kindness, formed of the purest dew and presented to the world as the most exquisite gem." Edward G. Browne contends that:

> Nizami's high rank as an original, fruitful, rare and noble genius is admitted by all critics, Persian and non-Persian, including Awfi, Gazwini, and Luft Ali Bey amongst biographers and Sadi, Hafiz, Jami, and Ismat amongst the poets. And if his genius has few rivals amongst the poets

191

SUFISM

of Persia, his character has even fewer. He was genuinely pious, yet singularly devoid of fanaticism and intolerance; self-respecting and independent, yet gentle and unostentatious; a loving father and husband. In a word, he may justly be described as combining lofty genius and blameless character in a degree unequalled by any other Persian poet.[1]

C. E. Wilson has offered a good description of Nizami's style: he uses a mode of expression which is rare, though not unique among Persian poets, who though often obscure, are generally what may be called conventionally obscure. Nizami, on the other hand, like many European poets, is unconventionally obscure. He employs images and metaphors to which there is no key save in the possession of the poetic sense and of sound judgment.

Dawlatshah, one of Nizami's Persian biographers, tells us that besides the "Treasury of Mysteries," *Khosrau and Shirin, Sikandar Nameh, Haft Payker* (The Seven Portraits), and *Laili and Majnun* (called "Khamsa" or "Quintet"), Nizami's odes, mystical poems and lyrical verses amounted to nearly twenty thousand verses, few of which, however, have come down to our times. Of Nizami's works available to us, *The Storehouse of Mysteries* is both the shortest and the earliest of the five books. It contains illustrative anecdotes after the fashion of Rumi's *Masnawi*. The following verses portray how people in power live in isolation and need wise and courageous advisers to tell them the truth and, if necessary, to rebuke them for their stupidity, injustice, neglect of duty, and failure to keep their word:

> Intent on sport, King Nushiravan on a day
> Suffered his horse to bear him far away
> From his retainers, only his vizier
> Rode with him, and no other soul was near.
> Crossing the game-stocked plain, he halts and scans

A village ruined as his foeman's plans.
There, close together, sat two owls apart,
Whose dreary hootings chilled the monarch's heart.
"What secrets do these whisper?" asked the King,
Of his vizier. "What means the song they sing?"
"O Liege," the minister replied, "I pray forgive me, for
   repeating what they say,
Not for the sake of song calls mate to mate:
A question of betrothal they debate
That bird his daughter gave to this, and now
Asks him a proper portion to allow,
Saying: "This ruined village give to me,
And also others like it two or three.'
'Let be,' the other cries; 'our rulers leave
Injustice to pursue, and do not grieve,
For if our worthy monarch should but live,
A hundred thousand ruined homes I'll give."[2]

In the romance of *Khosrau and Shirin*, which is the love
story of a Sassanian monarch, Khosrau Parviz, Nizami drew
from the sources used by the epic poet of Iran, Firdousi,
and other historians. Nizami's other work, *Iskandar-Namah*,
is a superb treatment of the legend of Alexander the Great
and his search for the Fountain of Life. According to
Nizami's biographers, this poem was written in two parts,
the first in 1191 and the second about 1200. The chief topic
is Nizami's description of Aristotle as the philosopher-
minister. In treating this subject, Nizami emphasizes, as
throughout his writings, the need of the just ruler for sound
and wise advice from a philosopher-vizier.

In 1198 Nizami composed *The Seven Beauties*. The hero of
this poem is the Sassanian monarch, Bahram Gur, whose
life history is recounted in the story. According to Nizami,
one day in a secret chamber in his castle Bahram discovers
the portraits of seven princesses of incomparable beauty.
These ladies were, respectively, the daughters of the King

of India, the Emperor of China, the Ruler of Kharazm, the King of the Slavs, the Emperor of Byzantium, the King of the West, and the Shah of the East. The romantic prince falls in love with all seven. As soon as his father dies and Bahram succeeds him, he demands and obtains from their fathers these seven princesses in marriage. Each wife, representing one of the seven climates into which Nizami's habitable world is divided, is lodged in a separate palace symbolically colored, and the King visits them on seven successive days, beginning on Saturday in the black palace assigned to the Indian princess and ending on Friday in the white palace in which the princess of the West (or sunset land) lives. Each of the seven princesses entertains the King in turn with tenderness, music, and love stories of her homeland. Some of the princesses also inform Bahram of the unjust deeds of his ministers and the suffering of the people.

Not satisfied with seven spouses, Bahram also has other mistresses. Nizami tells the story of one of these mistresses named Fitna ("Mischief") whom he used to take with him on his hunting expeditions where she would enchant him with the strains of the harp in which she was skilled. One day Bahram, who was very proud of his strength and skill in archery and hunting, chased a wild animal, expecting to win from his mistress an expression of admiration and a few words of praise, but:

> The maiden prompted by mere wantonness,
> Refused her admiration to express.
> The king was patient, till a wild ass broke
> Forth from its lair, then thus to her he spoke:
> "My skill, O Tartar maid, thy narrow eyes
> Behold not, or beholding to despise.
> My skill, which knoweth neither bound nor end,
> Entereth not thy narrow eyes, O friend.

Behold this beast, and bid my skill impale
When spot thou wilt between its head and tail,"
"Wouldst thou," said she, "thy skill to me make clear?
Then with one shaft transfix its hoof and ear."
The king, when this hard test was offered him,
Prepared to gratify her fancy's whim;
Called for a cross-bow, and forthwith did lay
Within the groove thereof a ball of clay.
Straight to the quarry's ear the pellet shot,
Whereat the beast, to sooth the smarting spot,
And to remove the clay, its foot on high
Did raise, whereon the king at once let fly
An arrow like a lightning flash, which sped
Straight to the hoof, and nailed it to the head.
Then to the maid of China said the king:
"Success is mine. What think you of this thing?"
"For long," said she, "the king this art hath wrought,
In tricks long practiced to succeed is naught.
What man hath studied long, he does with ease,
And solves the hardest problems, if he please.
That thus my lord the quarry's hoof should hit
Proves not so much his courage as his wit."[3]

Bahram, angered by his mistress's boldness, handed her
over to one of his generals to be put to death. The mistress,
being on good terms with the general, reminded him of the
favors she had done him. She also assured him that her
royal lover soon would be sorry for his hasty action and that
if he spared her life the king would be grateful to him. The
general, yielding to her entreaties, concealed her in his
hunting lodge in the mountains. In the dwelling was a long
staircase, and the king's mistress, determined to prove to
her lover that practice makes perfect, carried a newly-born
calf on her shoulders up and down the stairs every day, her
skill increasing with her practice. After the passage of many
months, the officer invited Bahram to his hunting lodge,
and the girl, veiling her face, seized the opportunity of

displaying her skill to her royal lover. The king, admiring this achievement, asked the girl to remove her veil. He was so happy to see his mistress alive and well that he praised the general for his wisdom and sagacity.

Nizami's celebrated work, the love story *Laili and Majnun,* is considered one of the greatest Persian classics. Few Persian poems have equaled this book in tenderness, grace, excitement, purity, and pathos. The beautiful work is compared to *Abelard and Eloise* and *Romeo and Juliet.* It is the account of a tragic love story, constantly referred to throughout the Middle East as an example of great devotion. The story is Arabic in origin, and it bears the impress of Arabic thought and psychology.

This poem contains the mystic lights and darknesses of life in the desert—the passionate love, the lofty aspirations and hopes, the dark disappointments, the unbearable grief, stoical patience, and invincible spirit which are characteristic of desert existence. Majnun, the lover, was the son of a rich and proud Arab chief; Laili, the daughter of a poor Bedouin, proud of his heritage and scornful of the chiefs and their religion. Laili is described as beautiful and enchanting, with rosy cheeks, black curly hair, ruby lips and teeth of pearl:

> When ringlets of a thousand curls
> And ruby lips and teeth of pearls
> And dark eyes flashing quick and bright,
> Like lightning on the bow of night—
> When charms like these this power display
> And steal the wildered heart away—
> Can man, dissembling, coldly seem
> Unmoved as by an idle dream?
> Kais saw her beauty and her grace
> The soft expression of her face;
> And as he gazed and gazed again
> Distraction stung his burning brain;

No rest he found by day or night
She was forever in his sight.[4]

But Laili's tribe soon folded their tents and moved to the
solitude of the mountains. They had left no trace, and as a
result, communication between the lover and the beloved
ended. The frantic Kais started an almost hopeless search
for his love. Laili had, with her kindred, been removed
among the Nijd mountains where she still cherished the
thoughts of him she loved, and her affection was even more
deeply aroused amidst that wild retreat.

Kais sought her there,
Sought her in rosy bower and silent glade,
Where the tall palm trees fling refreshing shade,
He called upon her name again;
Again, he called, alas in vain;
His voice unheard, though raised on every side;
Echo alone to his lament replied;
And Laili. Laili. Rang around,
As if enamoured of that magic sound.
Dejected and forlorn, fast-falling dew
Glisten'd upon his cheeks of pallid hue;
Through grove and frowning glen he lonely strayed,
And with his griefs the rocks were vocal made.
Beautiful Laili. Had she gone forever?
Could he that thought support? Oh, never, never.
Whilst deep emotion agonized his breast,
He to the morning breeze these words addressed:

"Breeze of the morn. So fresh and sweet,
Wilt thou my blooming mistress greet;
And nestling in her glossy hair,
My tenderest thoughts, my love, declare?
Wilt thou, while mid her tresses sporting;
Their odorous balm, their perfume courting,
Say to that soul-seducing maid,
In grief how prostrate I am laid.

And gently whisper in her ear
This message with an accent clear:

Thy figure is ever in my sight,
In thought by day, in dreams by night;
For one, in spirits sad and broken;
That mole will be the happiest token;
That mole which adds to every look
A magic spell I cannot brook;
For he who sees thy melting charms,
And does not feel his soul in arms,
Bursting with passion, rapture, all
That speak love's deepest, wildest thrall,
Must be, as *guaf's* ice-summit, cold,
And, happily scarce of human mould.
Let him, unmoved by charms like thine,
His worthless life at once resign—
Those lips are sugar, heavenly sweet,
Oh let but mine their pouting meet.
The balsam of delight they shed;
Their radiant colour ruby-red.
The evil eye has struck my heart,
But thine in beauty sped the dart:
Thus many a flower, of richest hue,
Hath fallen and perished where it grew;
Thy beauty is the sun in brightness,
Thy form a houri's self in lightness;
A treasure thou which poets say
The heavens would gladly steal away—
Too good, too pure, on earth to stay
If sympathy my heart incline,
Or vengeance, still the means are mine.
Treasure and arms can amply bear
Me through the toils of desert war;
But thou'rt the merchant peddler chief,
And I the buyer, come, sell, be brief.
If thou art wise, accept advice;
Sell and receive a princely price."[5]

Laili's proud father had defiantly told the chief that his
son was mad and therefore could not marry his daughter:

> Madness is neither sin, nor crime, we know,
> But who'd be linked to madness or foe?
> Thy son is mad—his senses first restore;
> In constant prayer the aid of heaven implore.
> But while portentous gloom pervades his brain
> Disturb me not with this vain suit again.
> The jewel sense no purchaser can buy,
> Nor treachery the place of sense supply.
> Thou hast my reasons and this parley o'er
> Keep them in mind and trouble me no more.

The despondent Majnun refuses to end his desperate
search and defies counsel and advice:

> Wanders near that palmy glade,
> Where the fresh breeze adds coolness to the shade?
> 'Tis Majnun—his ancestor's tomb,
> Again mid rocks and scorching plains to roam,
> Unmindful of the sun's meridian heat,
> Or the damp dewy night with unshod feet;
> Unmindful of the desert's savage brood,
> Howling on every side in quest of blood
> No dread has he from ought of earth or air,
> From den or aerie, calm in his despair:
> He seems to court new perils and can view
> With unblench'd visage scenes of darkest hue;
> Yet is he gentle, and his gracious mien
> Checks the extended claw, where blood has been;
> For tiger, wolf, and panther gather round
> The maniac as their king, and lick the ground;
> Fox and hyena fierce their snarling cease;
> Lion and fawn familiar meet in peace;
> Vulture and soaring eagle, on the wing,
> Around his place of rest their shadow fling;
> Like Solomon, o'er all extends his reign;
> His pillow is the lion's shaggy mane;

The wily leopard, on the herbage spread,
Forms like a carpet his romantic bed;
And lynx and wolf, in harmony combined,
Frisk o'er the sword, and gambol with the hind.
All pay their homage with respect profound,
As if in circles of enchantment bound.[6]

The kinsmen of Laili brought her the news that Majnun, insane and wild, was haunting the desert below the mountains and refused to go back to his own tribe. Laili blushed when she heard the news, but dared not venture forth to meet her crazed lover. Laili's father ordered some of his tribesmen to slay Majnun. When Majnun's father heard of this cruel and senseless step, he sent his own followers into the wilderness to rescue his son. Time after time Majnun was rescued and carried to his father's home, and as frequently he escaped and went back to the vicinity of the mountains where Laili's tribe had pitched their tents. Laili, hearing of all the tales of woe of her desperate lover became disconsolate.

Laili in beauty, softness, grace,
Surpassed the loveliest of her race
She was a fresh and odorous flower,
Pluck'd by a fairy from her bower,
With heart-delighting rosebuds blooming,
The welcome breeze of spring perfuming.
The killing witchery that lies
In her soft, black, delicious eyes,
When gathered in one amorous glance,
Pierces the heart, like sword and lance;
The prey that falls into her snare,
For life must mourn and struggle there;
Her eyelash speaks a thousand blisses,
Her lips of ruby ask for kisses;
Soft lips where sugar-sweetness dwell,
Sweet as the bee-hive's honey-cells;

Her cheeks, so beautiful and bright,
Had stolen the moon's beaming light;
Her form the cypress tree expresses,
And full and ripe invites caresses;
With all these charms the heart to win,
There was a careless grief within
Yet none beheld her grief, or heard;
She dropped like broken-winged bird.
Her secret thoughts her love concealing,
But, softly to the terrace stealing,
From morn to eve she gazed around,
In hopes her Majnun might be found,
Wandering in sight, for she had none
To sympathize with—not one.
None to compassionate her woes—
In dread of rivals, friends and foes;
And though she smiled, her mind's distress
Fill'd all thoughts with bitterness;
The fire of absence on them prey'd
But light nor smoke that fire betray'd;
Shut up within herself, she sate,
Absorbed in grief, disconsolate;
Yet though love has resources still,
In soothing arts, and ever will.[7]

An oasis with its cooling streams was near the mountains where Laili's tribe had their encampment. Here the gentle Laili came day after day, hoping to see her devoted lover. She gathered wild lilies and listened to the chirping of birds as she wandered through the fragrant groves. Alas, she could not find her Majnun. Then she reclined under a cypress tree and softly chanted her song of faithfulness:

"Oh faithful friend and lover true,
Still distraught from thy Laili's view,
Still absent, still beyond her power,
To bring thee to her fragrant bower;
Oh noble youth. Still thou art mine,
And Laili, Laili still is thine."

One day, as Laili sat under a cypress tree, a handsome young man suddenly appeared. His eyes rested a moment upon her crimson lips and the flowing dark tresses. He noticed too the full form with its shapely curves and the beaming softness of the dark eyes with their heavy lashes. The name of this young prince who had sought for a moment the cooling shade of the oasis trees was Ibn Salam. Seeing Laili, he fell in love and hastened to her father to ask for his daughter's hand. Dazzled by the position and wealth of the young prince, Laili's father gave a cordial consent to the union.

Meanwhile the chief of a neighboring tribe who knew Majnun's father and who had learned of the young man's pitiful loneliness and desperation, looked with compassion upon Majnun. With kindly words the chieftain soothed the restless lover. He received him in his tent and offered him care, clothes and food.

> An altered man, his mind at rest,
> In customary robes he dressed;
> A turban shades his forehead pale,
> No more is heard the lover's wail,
> His dungeon gloom exchanged for day,
> His cheeks a rosy tint display;
> He revels midst the garden sweets,
> And still his lip the goblet meets;
> But so intense his constant flame
> Each cup is quaffed in Laili's name.[8]

After entertaining Majnun for weeks, the generous chief decided to accompany the young man to the mountain fortress of Laili's tribe and to ask her father to allow Laili to marry Majnun. The obstinate father again haughtily refused and, as a result, a war broke out between the two tribes:

Arrows, like birds, on either foeman stood,
Drinking with open beak the vital flood;
The shining daggers in the battle's heat
Rolled many a head beneath the horse's feet;
And lightning herded by death's unsparing hand
Spread consternation through the weeping land.

The result of the conflict was disastrous for Laili's tribe:

And now the elders of that tribe appear,
And thus implore the victor chieftain, "Hear,
The work of slaughter is complete;
Thou seest our power destroyed; allow us
Wretched suppliants at thy feet
To humbly ask for mercy now.
How many warriors press the plain?
Dagger and spear have laid them low
At peace, behold our kinsman slain,
For thou art now without a foe.
Then pardon what of wrong has been;
Let us retire unharmed—unstay'd—
Far from this sanguine scene,
And take thy prize—the Arab maid."

The aged father came forth, admitting that his tribe was
completely vanquished. He offered the life of Laili as a
peace-offering to the victors, while still adamantly refusing
to allow her to wed the insane Majnun.

"My daughter shall be brought at they command;
The red flames may ascend from blazing brand
And slay their victim, crackling in the air,
And Laili dutiously shall perish there.
Or, if thou'dst rather see the maiden bleed,
This thirsty sword shall do the dreadful deed;
Sever at one blow that lovely head,
Her sinless blood by her own father shed.
In all things thou shall find me faithful, true,
Thy slave I am—what shouldst thou have me do?

But mark me; I am not to be beguiled;
I will not to a demon give my child;
I will not to a madman's wild embrace
Consign the pride, the pride and honor of my race;
And wed her to contempt and foul disgrace."[9]

The gallant chief, after listening to Laili's father, realized
that his purpose had been defeated and that many brave
men had shed their blood in vain. He at once issued an
order that the defeated and defiant tribe should be allowed
to retire unmolested from the field of battle.

"And thou and thine may quit the field.
Still armed with dagger, sword and shield;
Both horse and rider, thus in vain
Blood has bedewed this thirsty plain."

Then the brave chief, with a sad and heavy heart, pur-
sued his homeward way accompanied by the distressed and
desperate Majnun. He tried again to calm and console his
painful heart with fatherly care and gentleness.

But vain his efforts; mountain woods and plain
Soon heard the maniac's piercing woes again;
Escaped from listening ear and watchful eye,
Lonely again, in desert wild to lie.

Poor Laili, still in love with Majnun, listened to her
father's stubborn words forbidding her to meet Majnun or
communicate with anybody close to him. Meanwhile the
story of the beauty of Laili and the love of Majnun spread to
every oasis, and the neighboring tribes wondered who
would be the fortunate man to marry the beauty of Arabia.

2

At last Ibn Salam, Laili's betrothed, accompanied by his
rarest gems, the most expensive silk and golden robes,

magnificent carpets and hundreds of camels, arrived near the encampment of Laili's tribe. While the prenuptial rites engaged the chieftain's camp and every tent was filled with the tunes of the guitar, the voice of the flute, the sound of cymbals and the rattle of drums, the desolate Laili sat sad and lonely in her tent mourning her fate and pleading that she might be allowed to die rather than wed anybody but Majnun.

Laili's father ignored the pitiful pleadings of the girl and forced his daughter into a marriage which was only a fearful mockery. Laili refused to accept this farce and still cherished Majnun's memory with tenderest thought:

> Deep in her heart a thousand woes
> Disturbed her days and nights repose
> A serpent at its very core
> Writhing, gnawing evermore;
> And no relief—a prison room.
> Being now the lonely sufferer's doom.

In her prison Laili sat lonely and helpless, looking out upon the peaceful beauty of the night, watching the slow movement of the moon and stars. For days and months she lived within that guarded cell, shut like a gem within a stony bed, surrounded by watchmen assigned by her husband. After months of mental torture which seemed an eternity, one midnight Laili heard wailing cries and death chants outside her room.

Beneath her casement rang a wild lament, death-notes disturbed the night: The air was rent with clamorous voices; every hope had fled, he breathed no longer—Ibn Salam was dead.

> The fever's rage had ripp'd him in his bloom;
> He sank unloved, unpitied, to the tomb.

Laili looked up to the face of the moon and thought of

the chilling rays that fell upon the haggard form of her desert love. At this moment a delegation brought her the formal message that her so-called husband and jailer had died. Tribal custom required that she must mourn for the man she loathed and must assume the black garment of woe. It was easy for her to weep:

> But all the burning tears she shed
> Were for Majnun, not the dead.

The tribal law decreed that years must pass before freedom was given to the suffering Laili. But Laili, defying custom, arose one morning and told her faithful servant Zyd:

> "Today is not the day of hope,
> Which only gives to fancy scope;
> It is the day our hopes completing,
> It is the lover's day of meeting.
> Rise up. The world is full of joy;
> Rise up. And serve thy mistress, boy;
> Together, where the cypress grows,
> Place the red tulip and the rose;
> And let the long dissever'd meet—
> Two lovers, in communion sweet."

Then Laili, accompanied by her faithful servant, went to the grove of palms to meet her haggard lover. Sitting beside him, she laid her hand upon his arm, saying: "Ah, Majnun, it is thy Laili that has come to comfort you." Majnun's mind awoke with one glad cry, for the familiar voice with its caressing tones rang with the notes of heavenly joy. For one happy moment he embraced her and then, overcome with excitement, he fainted at her feet. Laili quickly knelt beside him, and then:

His head which in the dust was laid
Upon her lap she drew, and dried
His tears with tender hand and pressed
Him close and closer to her breast;
"Be here thy home beloved, adored,
Revive, be blest—Oh, Laili's lord."

At last he breathed, around he gazed,
As from her arms his head he raised—
"Art thou," he faintly said, "a friend
Who takes me to her gentle breast—
Dost thou in truth so fondly bend
Thine eyes upon a wretch distressed?

Are these thy unveiled cheeks I see
Can bliss be yet in store for me?
In sleep these transports I may share
But when I wake 'tis all despair.
Let me gaze on thee—e'en though it be
An empty shade alone I see;
How shall I bear what once I bore
When thou shalt vanish as before?"

The enchanting Laili rested in Majnun's arms, "with her dark ringlets flowing around her smooth neck, and the sweet confession of her love beaming in her tremulous eyes." Then Laili's tender words came to Majnun's ears:

"To hope, dear wanderer, revive;
Lo Zemzem[10], cool and bright,
Flows at thy feet—then drink and live
Seared heart. Be glad for bounteous heaven
At length our recompense hath given,
Beloved one, tell me all thy will
And know thy Laili faithful still.
Here in this desert, join our hands,
Our souls were joined long, long before;
And if our fate such doom demands,
Together wander evermore.

Oh Kais. Never let us part,
What is the world to thee and me?
My universe is where thou art
And is not Laili all to thee?"[11]

Majnun was faced with the greatest dilemma of his life.
He knew that he could not marry Laili according to the
tribal tradition, and his love for her was too pure and un-
selfish to accept Laili's proposal. After so many years of
suffering, was it right to push the tempting cup from his
thirsting lips? Should he accept the unfair and inhuman
tribal law and thus sacrifice the future of Laili and himself?
Were not all these laws made by unreasonable and au-
thoritarian chiefs? Did God require such a sacrifice after all
these years of loyalty and truth? Were they not already
wedded in His pure sight? Had she not always been his own
in the eyes of God and heaven? Should he outrage his own
conscience and sacrifice the honor of the woman whom he
loved with all his heart for the temporary enjoyment of this
life? His conscience and his tribal gallantry answered,
"Never." He clasped her closer to his bleeding heart—
kissed many times the tempting lips and then whispered:

"How well, how fatally I love,
My madness and my misery prove;
All earthly hopes I could resign—
Nay, life itself, to call thee mine.
But shall I make thy spotless name—
That sacred spell—a word of shame?

Shall selfish Majnun's heart be blest
And Laili prove the Arab's jest?
The city's gates though we may close
We cannot still our conscience's throes.
No—we have met—a moment's bliss
Has dawned upon my gloom in vain

Life yields no more a joy like this,
And all to come can be but pain.

Thou, thou, adored. Might be mine own
A thousand deaths let Majnun die
Ere but a breath by slander blown
Should sully Laili's purity.
Go, then—and to thy tribe return,
Fly from my arms that clasp thee yet;
I feel my brain with frenzy burn—
Oh, joy, could I but thus forget.

The fevered thoughts that on me prey
Death's sea alone can sweep away.
I found the bird of Paradise
That long I sought with care,
Fate snatched it from my longing eyes—
I held—despair.
Wail, Laili, wail our fortunes crossed,
Weep, Majnun, weep—forever lost."

Time passed by and no longer carried with it the flowers
of hope. No longer was the desert horizon illumed for the
two lovers with the rays of a happy future. Laili had spent
such a long time in the tower with despair and despondency
her only companions. Her life was empty, meaningless, and
there was nothing in this world which would keep her alive.
She called her mother to her side and expressed her last
wish before closing her eyes forever: "After my death,
please allow Majnun to weep over my grave."

It was now the task of Laili's faithful servant to find Maj-
nun and tell him of the death of his beloved: As soon as
Majnun heard the news he rushed to the grave of sweet
Laili:

And when the tomb of Laili meets his view,
Prostrate he falls, the grounds his tears bedew;

"Alas," he cries, "no more shall I behold
That angel face, that form of heavenly mould,
For thou hast quitted this contentious life,
This scene of endless treachery and strife
And I, like thee, shall soon my fetters burst,
And quench, in draughts of heavenly love, my thirst,
There where angelic bliss can never cloy,
We soon shall meet in everlasting joy;
The taper of our souls, more clear and bright,
Will then be lustrous with immortal light."[12]

A few days later Majnun's friends found him with his head lying lovingly upon her tomb, while upon his royal brow there rested the peaceful touch of death. His bleeding and broken heart had found rest at last, rest beyond the fevered dream of life with all its anxious hopes and fears. They opened Laili's tomb and laid the stilled heart beside her own:

> One promise bound their faithful hearts—
> One bed of cold, cold earth united them
> When dead. Severed in life, how cruel was
> Their doom. Ne'er to be joined but in the
>   Silent tomb.[13]

3

The faithful servant Zyd often wandered in the desert and pondered on the faith and devotion of the lovers. One night as he slept in the desert, looking at the shining stars, he saw the sands give way "to vistas of golden fruit and blooming roses; the white lilies gleamed amidst the green verdure. The nightingale sang in fadeless bowers, and the low, sweet voices of the ring-doves were heard among the feathery plumes of the palms. The desert voices gave way to the rich melodies from harp and shell. The fronded palms pressed upward, and a royal throne with gems and gold stood beneath their protecting shade."

The minstrel's legend-chronicle
Which on their woes delights to dwell,
Their matchless purity and faith,
And how their dust was mix'd in death,
Tells how the sorrow-stricken Zyd
Saw, in a dream, the beauteous bride,
With Majnun seated side by side.
In meditation deep, one night,
The other world flash'd on his sight
With endless vistas of delight—
The world of spirits;—as he lay
Angels appear'd in bright array,
Circles of glory round them gleaming,
Their eyes with holy rapture beaming,
He saw the ever-verdant bowers,
With golden fruit and blooming flowers;
The bulbul heard, their sweets among,
Warbling his rich mellifluous song;
The ring-dove's murmuring, and the swell
Of melody from harp and shell:
He was within a rosy glade,
Beneath a palm's extensive shade,
A throne, amazing to behold,
Studded with glittering gems and gold;
Celestial carpets near it spread
Close where a lucid streamlet stray'd;
Upon that throne, in blissful state,
The long-divided lovers sate,
Resplendent with seraphic light:—
They held a cup, with diamonds bright;
Their lips, by turns, with nectar wet,
In pure ambrosial kisses met;
Sometimes to each with tenderest feeling.
The dreamer who this vision saw
Demanded, with becoming awe,
What sacred names the happy pair
In Irem-bowers were wont to bear.
A voice replied: "That sparkling moon
Is Laili still—her friend, Majnun;
Deprived in your frail world of bliss,

They reap their great reward in this!"
Zyd, wakening from his wonderous dream,
Now dwelt upon the mystic theme,
And told to all how faithful love
Receives its recompense above.

The story of Zyd's glad vision spread throughout the
land, and has been repeated by scores of poets and in hundreds of songs written in Arabic, Persian, Urdu and Tur-
kish, narrating the sadness, the suffering, and the pure love
and nobility of Laili and Majnun.
Nizami concludes his story:

O ye, who thoughtlessly repose
On what this flattering world bestows,
Reflect how transient is your stay!
How soon e'en sorrow fades away!
The pangs of grief the heart may wring
In life, but Heaven removes the sting;
The world to come makes bliss secure,—
The world to come, eternal, pure.
What other solace for the human soul,
But everlasting rest—virtue's unvarying goal!
Saki! Nizami's strain is sung;
The Persian poet's pearls are strung;
Then fill again the goblet high!
Thou wouldst not ask the reveller why?
Fill to the love that changes never!
Fill to the love that lives forever!
That, purified by earthly woes,
At last with bliss seraphic glows.[14]

  1. Edward G. Browne, *A Literary History of Persia,* vol. II, T. Fisher, London,
1906, pp. 402–03.
  2. Translated by Edward G. Browne.
  3. Browne; vol. II, p. 410.
*Kais was the name of the son of the rich Arab chief who fell in love with Laili.
Laili's love drove Kais out of his mind, and he received the cognomen of Majnun
(crazy).
  4. Nizami, *Laili and Majnun,* translated by James Atkins, Bombay edition,
1821.

5. *Ibid.*, p. 163.
6. *Ibid.*, 140.
7. A. J. Arberry, *Persian Poems*, Everyman's Library, New York, pp. 149–60.
8. *Ibid.*
9. Nizami, *Laili and Majnun, op. cit.*
10. Zemzem is the sacred well enclosed by the temple at Mecca, and even a stone dipped in its waters is thought to possess marvelous virtues.
11. Nizami, *Laili and Majnun, op. cit.*
12. Arberry, *op. cit.*, pp. 155–56.
13. *Ibid.*
14. Elizabeth A. Reed, *Persian Literature*, S. C. Griggs and Company, 1893, pp. 294–08.

9

Omar Khayyam, the Conscience of Sufism

The Moving Finger writes; and, having writ,
Moves on; nor all Your Piety nor Wit
Shall lure it back to cancel half a Line
Nor all Your Tears wash out a Word of it.
                    The Rubaiyat of Omar Khayyam

Ghias Uddin Abul Fath Omar Ibrahim al Khayyam, the son of a tentmaker, was born about A.D. 1044 in Nishapur, Khurasan, and died about 1124. As a young man he studied under famous scholars at Nishapur[1] and gained a remarkable knowledge of the Arabic language, Islamic and Greek philosophy, history, theology, astronomy, and mathematics. It was Omar who devised for Sultan Malek Shah the Persian calendar, which is considered by historians, including Edward Gibbon, as more accurate than either the Julian or Gregorian, and which is still in official use in Iran.

Apart from his world-famous *Rubaiyat*, Omar also wrote the *Noruz Namah* (the Persian New Year), a history of the

214

Persian New Year festival commencing with the first day of spring, in which he tells the story of how the Persians discovered wine. He is, in addition, the author of an algebraic tract in Arabic, a book on geometry, essays on mathematics, meteorology and metaphysics, and philosophical treatises based on the works of Avicenna, the great Persian philosopher and physician. Omar was an astronomer and mathematician by vocation and a poet by avocation. His poetry needs no introduction to the English-speaking world, for it was brought from obscurity to international fame by Edward FitzGerald, the British poet and translator.

Alfred Lord Tennyson paid FitzGerald the ultimate tribute with the following verse, with which the world has ever since agreed:

> Who reads your golden Eastern lay,
> Than which I know no version done
> In English more divinely well;
> A planet equal to the sun
> Which cast it, that large infidel
> Your Omar; and your Omar drew
> Full-handed plaudits from our best
> In modern letter.

John Ruskin, the English essayist and critic, told Fitz-Gerald: "I do not know in the least who you are, but I do with all my soul pray you find and translate some more of Omar Khayyam for us: I never did—till this day—read anything so glorious, to my mind, as this poem (10th, 12th pages, if one were to choose) and that, and this, is all I can say about it—more—more—please more—and that I am ever gratefully and respectfully yours."

It has been suggested that Omar's poetry is religious allegory. This false assumption has arisen for two reasons:

the lack of research and objective criticism and the belief that Omar, as a Sufi, must have believed that "the individual soul, once part of God, could find salvation in being reabsorbed in Him again *after renunciation of all earthly desires and pleasures.*"

As a Sufi, Omar did accept the renunciation of greed and worldly ambition, but he was a true human being who hated hypocrisy and dishonesty and expressed his opinion clearly, frankly, and honestly:

> And this I know! Whether the one true light,
> Kindle to Love, or wrath consume me quite,
> One glimpse of it within the tavern caught
> Better than in the temple lost outright.
> Some people are meditating upon doctrine and faith
> One group are bewildered about doubt and certainty;
> Suddenly a proclamation emerges from a hiding place,
> "O ignorant ones, the way is neither that nor this.'
>
> My coming was not of mine own design,
> And one day I must go, and no choice of mine;
> Come, light-handed cup-bearer, gird thee to serve,
> We must wash down the care of this world with wine."[2]

The Sufis maintain that there are four different paths people may take in their lives:

1. The way of material life. By profession, by occupation, business, or industry, a person wants to make money and attain power.

2. The way of duty—to our community, town, country, or our fellow men. The sense of duty is a great virtue, and when it is perfected and deepened in the heart of a man it wakens him to a greater and higher consciousness.

3. The way of universal consciousness—through love of others, through world brotherhood, and through service. This is the way of those who consider life a swiftly passing

dream. Ask a man who has lived a hundred years, "What do you think about life on earth?" and he will say, "one night's dream, my child, it is no longer than that." Therefore the ultimate purpose which the soul seeks every moment of life is spiritual salvation.

4. The last way is to make the best of the time and opportunity given to us on this earth, and it is this point of view that Omar stressed intensely:

XXI

Ah My Beloved, fill the Cup that clears
To-day of past Regrets and future Fears:
To-morrow—Why, To-morrow I may be
Myself with Yesterday's Sev'n thousand Years![3]

Omar was hated and dreaded by religious fanatics because he attacked their hypocrisy and ignorance and their use of religion for their own personal interests. He rejected the concepts of Heaven and Hell which he claimed were invented to keep mankind in the bonds of the clergy of every religion.

Omar was too honest of heart as well as of head for this. Having failed (however mistakenly) of finding any providence but destiny, and any world but this, he set about making the most of it; preferring rather to soothe the soul through the senses into acquiescence with things as they were, than to perplex it with vain mortifications after what they might be. It has been seen that his worldly desires, however, were not exorbitant; and he very likely takes a humorous pleasure in exaggerating them above that intellect in whose exercise he must have found great pleasure, though not in a theological direction. However, this may be, his worldly pleasures are what they profess to be without any pretense at divine allegory: his wine is the veritable juice of the grape: his tavern, where it was to be

had; *his saki,* the flesh and blood that poured it out for
him; all of which are real, and where the roses were in
bloom was everything he professed to want of this world
or to expect of paradise.

XII

A Book of Verses underneath
  the Bough,
A Jug of Wine, a Loaf
  of Bread—and Thou
Beside me singing in
  the Wilderness—
Oh, Wilderness were Paradise enow!

XXVII

Myself when young did eagerly frequent
Doctor and Saint, and heard great argument
About it and about: but evermore
Came out by the same door wherein I went.[4]

Omar's heaven was of this world, and he idealized the
Hindu vision of Paradise as music, love, singing, playing,
and dancing. Hell was avarice, greed, tyranny, and the
exploitation of man by his fellow man. To Omar Khayyam
universal joy and love constituted the supreme religion of
man upon which all creeds should be based. His mysticism
reveals the possibility of a nobler, happier and freer human
nature. Virtue and vice, according to Omar, and even the
higher good that mysticism finds everywhere, are the reflec-
tions of our emotions on other things, not part of the substance of things as they are in themselves:

XVI

I sent my soul through the Invisible,
Some by letter of that After-life to spell:

And by and by my soul return'd to me,
And answered "I myself am Heav'n and Hell."

XIII

Some for the glories of this world, and some
Sigh for the prophet's paradise to come;
Ah, take the cash, and let the credit go,
Nor heed the rumble of a distant drum![5]

If you can lay hands on a jar of wine,
Drink from it where you gather with your friends;
For he who made the world has little use
For all our petty airs and vanities.

XXV

Alike for those who for today prepare,
And those that at tomorrow stare,
A Muezzin from the tower of darkness cries,
'Fools! Your reward is neither here nor there!'

2

It is very strange that none of Omar's contemporaries
have mentioned him as a poet. The oldest account of Omar
by Nizami Aruzi, who was personally acquainted with him,
never mentions Omar's poetry:

> At the year A.H. 506 [A.D. 1112–1113] Khwaja Imam
> Omar-i-Khayyami and Khawja Imam Muzaffar arrived
> in the city of Balkj, in the street of slave sellers, in the
> house of Amir Abu Sad Jarrah. I had the pleasure of
> joining that assembly. In the midst of our convivial
> gathering, I heard Omar saying, 'My grave will be in a
> spot where the trees will shed their blossoms on me twice
> a year.' This seemed to me impossible, thought I knew
> that a man like Omar would not speak idle words.

When I arrived in Nishapour in the year A.D. 1136,

four years after the death of that great man [Omar] I
went to visit his grave on a Friday evening. A guide took
me to Hira Cemetery. I found Omar's tomb situated at
the foot of a garden wall, over which pear trees and
peach trees thrust their branches and on his grave had
fallen so many flower leaves that his dust was hidden
beneath the flowers. Then I remembered that saying
which I had heard from him in the city of Balkh, and
started to weep. Because on the face of the earth, and all
the regions of the habitable globe, I never saw one like
him.

Although I witnessed this prophecy on the part of the
Proof of the Truth [Omar], I did not observe that he personally believed in astrological predictions."[6]

"Mirshadul-Ebad," composed in A.D. 1234, contains a
passage in which Omar for the first time is mentioned in
connection with his poetry. He is denounced as an atheist,
and two of his quatrains are cited with disapproval:

But those poor philosophers, atheists and materialists,
who are debarred from these two stations, err and go
astray, so that one of the most talented of them, who is
known and noted amongst them for scholarship,
philosophical knowledge and judgment, that is Omar
Khayyam, in the extreme of bewilderment must need
advertise his blindness in the desert of error by uttering
the following verses:

To that circle wherein is our coming and going
Neither beginning nor end is apparent
No one breathes a true word in this world
As to whence is our coming and whither our going.
Since (God the All) holder arranged the composition of
    men's natures
Wherefore did He again cast them into decline and decay?
If these forms are ugly, whose is the fault,
And if they are good, wherefore their destruction?[7]

Qifti, a historian of the second quarter of the thirteenth century, refers to Omar in his history of philosophers as a "champion of Greek learning" (i.e., philosophy), of which the great mystic, Jalalud-Din Rumi says in his *Mathnawi:*

"How long (will ye talk of) the philosophy of the Greeks?
Study also the philosophy of these of the faith."

Futhermore, Qifti states that the later Sufis "found themselves in agreement with some part of the apparent sense of [Omar's] verse, and have transferred it to their system, and discussed it in their assemblies and private gatherings; though its inward meanings are to the [ecclesiastical] law stinging serpents, and combinations rife with malice. He was without an equal in astronomy and philosophy but an advanced thinker, constrained only by prudential motives to bridle his tongue."[8]

Another book, *Tarikh-i-Alfi,* published in A.D. 1591, refers to Omar in the following words:

It appears from numerous books that he [Omar] held the doctrine of metempsychosis. It is related that there was in Nishapur an old college, for the repairing of which donkeys were bringing bricks. One day, while the sage Omar was walking with a group of students, one of the donkeys would on no account enter the college. When Omar saw this, he smiled, went up to the donkey, and extemporized the following quatrain:

O lost and now returned yet more astray,
Thy name from men's remembrance passed away,
Thy nails have now combined to form thy hoofs,
Thy tail's a beard turned round the other way.

The donkey then entered, and they asked Omar the reason for this. He replied, "The spirit which has now attached itself to the body of this ass [formerly] inhabited the body of a lecturer in this college, therefore it would not come in until now, when, perceiving that its colleagues had recognized it, it was obliged to step inside."⁹

The oldest manuscript of the *Rubaiyat* (Omar's quatrains) was copied in A.D. 1460, nearly three and one-half centuries after Omar's death. The text of this, in facsimile, with literal prose translation, was published by Edward Heron Allen in London, in 1898.

How many *Rubaiyats* attributed to Omar are really his is impossible to say, since no manuscript before A.D. 1460 has been discovered. Some Orientalists and Persian scholars have attributed more than eighty of the quatrains to Abu Said, Ghazali, Razi, Avecenna, Rumi, and other poets. The oldest manuscript contains only 158 quatrains. But John Payne's (1842–1916) metrical translation of all available *Rubaiyats* attributed to Omar exceed twelve hundred quatrains.¹⁰

As for FitzGerald's translation or paraphrase, compared with the original, according to Edward G. Browne, this point has been exhaustively worked out, and the conclusion is that, of FitzGerald's translations, forty-nine are faithful and beautiful paraphrases of single quatrains to be found in the Calcutta manuscript. Forty-four are traceable to more than one quatrain, and may therefore be termed the "composite" quatrains. Two are inspired by quatrains found by FitzGerald only in Nicola's text. Two are quatrains reflecting the whole spirit of the original poem. Two are traceable exclusively to the influence of Attar. Two quatrains primarily inspired by Omar influenced the odes of Hafiz. And three, which appeared only in the first and second edition of FitzGerald's translation and were later omitted from other editions are not attributable to any lines of the original texts.¹¹

Although the *Rubaiyat* has been repeatedly printed in
Iran and India, they enjoy, thanks to FitzGerald's translation, a far greater celebrity in the West, especially in England; in Iran no one would think of ranking Omar as a
poet in the same category as Firdawsi, Sadi, or Hafiz. The
reasons for Omar's popularity in the West, according to
Browne, are manifold. First, he had the supreme good fortune to find a translator like FitzGerald. Second, the beauty
of his quatrains depends more on their substance rather
than on their form, whereas the converse holds true for
much Persian poetry. Third, their gentle melancholy, half-
skeptical mysticism and graceful pessimism are congenial to
an age which, like his own, has come to the conclusion that
science can answer almost every question save that which
most intimately concerns our own hopes and happiness.[12]

13

Omar's criticism of his society produced many enemies
who called him "an unhappy philosopher, atheist, ma-
terialist, and enemy of religion." In answer to these ac-
cusations Omar replied:

Those men who lay the foundation of their virtue
Upon hypocrisy, they commit the error of making
Distinction between body and soul: henceforth I will
Set the goblet of wine upon my head, even if, like a
Cock, they set a saw upon my crown [slay me].

We made the wine-jar's lip our place of prayer
And drink in lessons of manhood there,
And pass our lives in taverns, if perchance
The time misspent in mosques we may repair.

Am I a wine-bibber? What if I am?
A lover, or idolatrous? Suppose I am?

Each sect miscalls me, but I heed them not,
I am my own, and what I am, I am.

O city Mufti, you more astray
Than I, although to drinking I give way;
I drink the blood of grapes, you that of men:
Which of us is the more bloodthirsty, pray?

Though I drink wine, I am no libertine,
Nor am I grasping, save of cups of wine;
You ask me why I worship wine? Because
To worship self, like you, I still decline.[13]

It is sometimes asked why Omar sounds different from
many Persian Sufi poets. The answer is very difficult, but
a guess is that it is found in his temperament and back-
ground. Omar's first loves were science, Greek philosophy,
and Islamic theology; yet the more he studied, the less
spiritual and intellectual satisfaction he received.

When his brilliant mind confronted the same intellectual
and spiritual disappointment that faced Al-Ghazali, he rejected both authority-based beliefs and worldly power and
pomp. As a result he turned to mysticism as the most likely
path to the truth he was seeking—as a kind of catalyst
between formalism and philosophy:

Being and Nothing alike I know,
Essence of things above and things below,
But,—shame upon my knowledge!—to be drunk
Is after all the highest lore I know.

They who, renowned for love and power of brain,
As "guiding lights" men's homage did obtain,
Not even they emerged from this dark night,
But told their dreams, and fell asleep again.[14]

If thy labor is in quest of enough worldly
substance to feed and to clothe thyself

withal, thou art excused. The rest is worthless;
beware not trade thy precious life for all that.[15]

'Tis all a chequer-board of nights and days
Where destiny with men for pieces plays:
Hither and thither moves, and mates and slays,
and one by one back in the closet lays.[16]

Omar was pained by the decadence of contemporary Sufi
life, and in expressing his misgivings and objections, he was
accused of heresy. One of his important accomplishments
was to exemplify a new kind of Sufi, free from the concept
of Sufism as a full-time vocation. He achieved this by viewing Sufism as a state of mind, devoid of hypocrisy, hatred,
greed and deceit. Neither a dry ascetic nor a hypocritical
theologian, he abandoned pomp and power and adopted
the ways of the mystics. Oblivious to the material world,
Omar lost himself in his garden, rising above worldly gain,
wondering at man's anguish and rejoicing in his discovery
of the human and divine realities of kindness, care, and
consideration.

The problems of poverty, inequity, war, and feuds, con-
spicuous in Omar's time, pained him greatly. Contemplat-
ing the destiny of people, he could suddenly plunge into a
state of sorrow and helplessness after having been jovial
and having entertained some moments of happiness:

What is this world? A caravanserai,
The haunt of alternating night and day,
The leavings of a hundred Jamshid's feasts,
The couch whereon a hundred Bahrams lay!

Ask not the chances of futurity,
Nor grieve for joys that now are lost to thee;
Set down as gain this ready-money breath!
Forget the past, and let the future be.

Man, like a ball, hither and thither goes,
As the strong bat of fate directs the blows;
But He, who gave thee up to this rude sport,
He knows what drives thee, yea, He knows, He knows![17]

Seek not after happiness, for the produce of life
is [but] a breath; every mote is [made up] of
the dust of Kaikobad and a Jamshid: the circumstances
of the world, nay, the universe entire, are [but]
a sleep and a dream, a deceit and a delusion.[18]

To Sir Gore Ouseley, Omar was:

altogether unprecedented in regard to the freedom of his
religious opinions; or rather, his boldness in denouncing
hypocrisy and indolence, and enlightened views he took
of the fanaticism and mistaken devotion of his countrymen. He may be called the Voltaire of Persia; though his
writings are not calculated to shock European notions so
much as those of the followers of the Prophet. The
priests were his great enemies, and he was peculiarly
hated by false devotees, whose acts he exposed. His in-
dulgence to other creeds gave great offence, and his liberty of speech drew down upon him continued censure;
yet was he extremely popular, and his compositions were
read with avidity by those who did not come under the
head of bigots, and the admiration of this class consoled
him for the enmity of the other.

Ye, who seek for pious fame,
And that light should gild your name,
Be this duty ne'er forgot,—
Love your neighbor—harm him not.
To thee, great spirit, I appeal,
Who canst the gates of truth unseal;
I follow none, nor ask the way
Of men who go, like me, astray;
They perish, but Thou canst not die,
But liv'st to all eternity.
Such is vain man's uncertain state,

A little makes him base or great;
One hand shall hold the Koran's scroll,
The other raise the sparkling bowl—
One saves, and one condemns the soul.[19]

The temple I frequent is high,
A turquoise-vaulted dome—the sky,
That spans the worlds with majesty,
Not quite a Moslem is my creed,
Quite an infidel; my faith, indeed,
May startle some who hear me say,
I'd give my pilgrim staff away,
And sell my turban, for an hour
Of music in a fair one's bower.
I'd sell the rosary for wine,
Though holy names around it twine.

And prayers the pious make so long
Are turned by me to joyous song;
Or, if a prayer I should repeat,
It is at my beloved's feet.

They blame me that my words are clear;
Because I am what I appear;
Nor do my acts my words belie—
At least, I shun hypocrisy
I marked a potter beating clay
The earth spoke out—"Why dost thou strike?
Both thou and I are born alike;
Though some may sink and some may soar,
We all are earth, and nothing more."

Nature made me love the rose,
And my hand was formed alone
Thus the wine cup to enclose;
Blame them—ye, the goblet's foes,—
Nature's fault and not my own.
When a houri form appears,
Which a vase of ruby bears,
Call me infidel if then I prize
All the joys of paradise.

Why ungrateful man—repine,
When this cup is bright with wine?
All my life I've sought in vain,
Knowledge and content to gain;
All that nature could unfold,
Have I in her page unrolled;
All of glorious and grand
I have sought to understand.
'Twas in youth my early thought,
Riper years no wisdom brought,
Life is ebbing, sure though slow,
And I feel I nothing know.

Bring the bowl! at least in this,
Dwells no shadowed distant bliss;
See I clasp the cup whose power
Yields more wisdom in an hour
Than whole years of study give,
Vainly seeking how to live.

Wine dispenses into air!
Selfish thought and selfish care,
Dost thou know why wine I prize?
He who drinks all ill defies:
And can awhile throw off the thrall
Of self, the God we worship—all!

All we see—above, around—
Is but built on fairy ground:
All we trust is empty shade
To deceive our reason made.
Tell me not of paradise,
Or the beams of houri's eyes;
Who the truth of tales can tell,
Cunning priests invent so well?
He who leaves this mortal shore,
Quits it to return no more.

In vast life's unbounded tide
They alone content may gain,

Who can good from ill divide,
Or in ignorance abide—
All between is restless pain.
Before thy prescience, power divine
What is this idle sense of mine?
What all the learning of the schools?
What sages, priests, and pedants? fools?
The world is thine, from thee it rose,
By thee it ebbs, by thee it flows.
Hence, worldly lore by whom is wisdom shown?
The eternal knows, knows all and He alone![20]

So much care for wealth and regret for worldly goods—
What is it? Hast thou ever seen any man who lived eternally?
These few breaths in thy body are [but] a loan;
With a thing loaned, one must live as a thing transient.[21]

Drunkards are doomed to hell, so I declare,
Believe it not, 'tis but a foolish scare;
Heaven will be empty as this hand of mine,
If none who love good drink find entrance there.

Khayyam! Why weep you that your life is bad?
What boots it thus to mourn? Rather be glad.
He that sins not can make no claim to mercy.
Mercy was made for sinners—be not sad.

To drain the cup, to hover round the fair—
Can hypocritic arts with these compare?
If all who love and drink are bound for hell,
There's many a wight of heaven may well despair![22]

XCIX

Ah Love! could you and I with Him conspire
To grasp this sorry Scheme of Things entire,
Would not we shatter it to bits—and then
Re-mold it nearer to the Heart's Desire![23]

Small gains to learning on this earth accrue,
They pluck life's fruitage, learning who eschew;
Take pattern by the fools who learning shun,
And then perchance shall fortune smile on you.

Did he who made me fashion me for hell,
Or destine me for heaven? I cannot tell.
Yet will I not renounce cup, lute and love,
Nor earthly cash for heavenly credit sell.

If God wills me not to will aright,
How can I frame my will to will aright?
Each single act I will must needs be wrong.
Since none but He can make me will aright.[24]

Omar's poetry is a reaction to an atmosphere of intolerance, cruelty, hypocrisy, oppression, and virtual lack of religious or political freedom. There is something contradictory about Persia. While its literature and culture are in the best tradition of tolerance, humanitarianism, compassion, brotherhood and universalism, some of its political and religious establishments have been oppressive, unwilling to endure opposition, lacking in respect for individual rights and intolerant of new or progressive ideas. People accused of religious or political heresies have been imprisoned, banished, and executed. Omar, Hafiz, Hallaj, and thousands of other writers, poets, and political thinkers have revolted against this stifling and strangling system. The driving force of this rebellion has undoubtedly been intellectual restlessness. From early youth, confesses Omar, his mind had no rest, for his soul perceived the atmosphere of hypocrisy and deceit, and the cannibalism of his time:

Heaven multiplies our sorrows day by day,
And grants no joys it does not take away;
If those unborn could know the ills we bear,
What think you, would they rather come or stay?[25]

As I see the affairs of the universe, I see
How worthless the whole world is in that respect;
God be praised, that in all that I behold
I see nothing but my own disappointment.

Be not disheartened; perform your duty; share
with others whatever you possess; do not violate
life and property of any man; concerning the other
world I guarantee your salvation—Bring wine.

O Fortune, thou confessest thy own tyrannies;
Thou art immured in the monastery of injustice
and oppression: To worthless men thou givest
wealth, to prominent men, suffering—it must be
one of these two, either thou art an ass, or a dotard.[26]

4

Khayyam attempted throughout his life to convince his
readers that mysticism was not an exclusive cult but a way of
life common to all the religions of the world. He lamented
the fact that people fought in the name of religious rites
and rituals and, like mad dogs, destroyed everything decent
and sacred.

According to Omar there is truth in every religion, and it
is wrong to claim that ours is the only God or the only
scripture, or that our place of worship is the only abode of
God. In Omar's time, every sheikh, priest, king, courtier,
and theologian claimed his religion to be the best and,
therefore, arrogated to himself the right to deprive others
of their freedom of worship. Omar felt that such intolerance was against the laws of God and nature, and he chal-
lenged the theologians and priests to practice what they
were preaching. His mysticism was a protest against the
tyrant and the oppressor. By tolerating all, he did not belong to a religion, but all religions belonged to him. He

viewed all creeds as free expressions of beliefs which have
one fundamental command in common:

> Heed not traditions, forms, or discipline;
> so that you injure none and none malign;
> And ne'er withhold your store from worthy men,
> I guarantee you heaven—and now some wine.
>
> My beloved—may her life be as long as my sorrow!—
> Today she renewed her affection; for a moment
> Darted a glance from her eyes, and then she passed
> And said, 'Do good and cast it on the water.'[27]

Omar Khayyam constantly endeavored to draw attention
to the factors which had caused misery, poverty, oppression, and unhappiness in Persia. He could not and dared
not criticize the Sultan, the religious, or the establishment
leaders directly, so he blamed "the wheels of fortune," "destiny," "providence," the Sufis, and the ascetics.

Ultimately, though, Omar moved away from the court
and the Church. Certainly the ravages of despotism and
religious fanaticism he had witnessed in the realm influenced his judgment, for he considered blind submis-
sion to the despotic Shah, his corrupt court, and the hypocritical clergy a crude form of idolatry, a deification of op-
pressors. Religious intolerance and proselytism were to him
not only an affront to human intelligence but also contrary
to universal brotherhood.

To Omar there was only one human community, and the
pressure on the people to follow Islam alone was unaccept-
able. "Look at the history of mankind," he told his readers.
"It is an unending succession of deadly combat, bloody
feuds, religious persecution, human exploitation, and war."
To him the issue was clear and not arguable: Leave people
freedom of choice in their religion and way of life. They are
born free and must stay free.

Omar spoke to the whole world: All men and women, regardless of creed, race, and color, belonged to the Kingdom of God on this earth and were entitled to happiness and harmony. In his endeavor to make a case for world brotherhood and individual freedom, he reminded his society of the transient nature of power, pomp, and erudition:

X

But come with old Khayyam, leave the lot
Kaikobad and Kaikhosru forgot:[28]
Let Rustun lay about him as he will,
or Hatim Tai 'To supper!' Heed them not.[29]

Every place where there has been a rose and a tulip bed
It has come from the redness of some prince's blood;
Every violet-shoot that grows out of the earth
Is a mole that was once on the cheek of some beauty.

Be prudent, for fortune stirs up much trouble;
Sit not secure, for the sword of destiny is sharp.
If fate should place a sugar-almond in your palate,
Beware do not swallow it, for it is mixed with poison.

XVI

Think, in this batter'd Caravanserai
Whose doorways are alternate Night and Day,
How Sultan after Sultan with his Pomp
Abode his Hour or two, and went his way.

XXVI

Why, all the saints and sages who discussed
Of the two worlds so learnedly, are thrust
Like foolish prophets forth; their words to scorn
Are scatter'd and their mouths are stopt with dust.[30]

XXIV

Ah, make the most of what we yet may spend,
Before we too into the Dust descend:
    Dust into Dust, and under Dust, to lie,
Sans Wine, sans Song, sans Singer, and—sans End!

XXXIV

Then of the Thee in Me who works behind
The Veil, I lifted up my hands to find
    A lamp amid the Darkness; and I heard,
As from Without: "The Me within Thee Blind!"

XLI

Perplext no more with Human or Divine,
To-morrow's tangle to the winds resign,
    And lose your fingers in the tresses of
The Cypress-slender Minister of Wine.

LV

You know, my Friends, with what a brave Carouse
I made a Second Marriage in my house;
    Divorced old barren Reason from my Bed,
And took the Daughter of the Vine to Spouse.

LVII

Ah, but my Computations, People say,
Reduced the Year to better reckoning?—Nay,
    'Twas only striking from the Calendar
Unborn To-morrow, and dead Yesterday.

LVIII

And lately, by the Tavern Door agape,
Came shining through the Dusk an Angel Shape
    Bearing a Vessel on his Shoulder; and
He bid me taste of it; and 'twas—the Grape!

LIX

The Grape that can with Logic absolute
The Two-and-Seventy jarring Sects confute:
    The sovereign Alchemist that in a trice
Life's leaden metal into Gold transmute;

LXIV

Strange, is it not? that of the myriads who
Before us pass'd the door of Darkness through,
    Not one returns to tell us of the Road,
Which to discover we must travel too.

LXV

The Revelations of Devout and Learn'd
Who rose before us, and as Prophets burn'd,
    Are all but Stories, which, awoke from Sleep,
They told their comrades, and to Sleep return'd.

LXVI

I sent my Soul through the Invisible,
Some letter of that After-life to spell:
    And by and by my Soul return'd to me,
And answer'd: "I Myself am Heav'n and Hell"

LXVIII

We are no other than a moving row
Of Magic Shadow-shapes that come and go
    Round with the Sun-illumined Lantern held
In Midnight by the Master of the Show;

LXXIV

YESTERDAY *This* Day's Madness did prepare;
TO-MORROW's Silence, Triumph, or Despair:
    Drink! for you know not whence you came, nor why:
Drink! for you know not why you go nor where.

LXXVI

The Vine had struck a fiber: which about
If clings my Being—let the Dervish flout;
   Of my Base metal may be filed a Key,
That shall unlock the Door he howls without.

LXXX

O Thou, who didst with pitfall and with gin
Beset the Road I was to wander in,
   Thou wilt not with Predestined Evil round
Enmesh, and then impute my Fall to Sin!

LXXXI

O Thou, who Man of baser Earth didst make
And ev'n with Paradise devise the Snake:
   For all the Sin wherewith the Face of Man
Is blacken'd—Man's forgiveness give—and take!

Said one among them—"Surely not in vain
My substance of the common Earth was ta'en
   And to this Figure molded, to be broke,
Or trampled back to shapeless Earth again."

LXXXVI

After a momentary silence spake
Some Vessel of a more ungainly Make;
   "They sneer at me for leaning all awry:
What! did the Hand then of the Potter shake?"

XCII

That ev'n my buried Ashes such a snare
Of Vintage shall fling up into the Air,
   As not a True-believer passing by
But shall be overtaken unaware.

XCVI

Yet Ah, that Spring should vanish with the Rose!
That Youth's sweet-scented manuscript should close!
   The Nightingale that in the branches sang,
Ah whence, and whither flown again, who knows!

C

Yon rising Moon that looks for us again—
how oft hereafter will she wax and wane;
   How oft hereafter rising look for us
Through this same Garden—and for *one* in vain!

CI

And when like her, O Sákí, you shall pass
Among the Guests Star-scatter'd on the Grass,
   And in your joyous errand reach the spot
Where I made One—turn down an empty Glass![31]

In his first introduction to the translation of the *Rubaiyat,* FitzGerald compares Omar to Lucretius, both in natural temper and genius. He considers them both men of subtle intellect and high imagination, "instructed in learning beyond their day, [with] hearts passionate for truth and justice;" who justly revolted against the hypocrisy and falsehood of their time. While Lucretius consoled himself with a stoical attitude, Omar, more desperate, "flung his own genius and learning into the general ruin which their insufficient glimpses only served to reveal, and, yielding his senses to the actual rose and wine, only diverted his thoughts by balancing ideal possibilities of fate, freewill, existence and annihilation:"[32]

   Oh, if my soul can fling his dust aside,
   And naked on the air of Heaven rise,

Is't not a shame, is't not a shame for Him
So long in this clay suburb to abide.

Or is that but a tent, where rests anon
A sultan to his kingdom passing on,
And which the swarthy chamberlain shall strike
Then when the sultan rises to be gone.[33]

LXXII

Alas, that spring should vanish with the rose!
That youth's sweet-scented manuscript should close!
The nightingale that in the Branches sang
Ah, whence and whither flown again, who knows!

LXXIII

Ah love! Could thou and I with fate conspire
To grasp this story scheme of things entire,
Would not we shatter it to bits—and then
Re-mould it nearer to the heart's desire!

LXXV

And when thyself with shining foot shall pass
Among the guests star-scatter'd on the grass,
And in thy joyous errand reach the spot
Where I made one—turn down an empty glass![34]

1. FitzGerald, in his biography, tells a story taken from an early fourteenth-century work, the *Jami ul Tavarikh* of Rashid'ud-Din Fazlullah, a history of the Mongols, including a section on the general history of Persia. Omar, he relates, was one of three pupils of the Imam Mowaqu of Nishapur, the other two being Nizam ul Mulk and Hassan Sabbah. The three pledged that they would share whatever power and prosperity they achieved. Later on when Nizam ul Mulk became chancellor of the realm, Omar did not ask for any favor, but Hassan Sabbah came to claim a place in the government as his share of his friend's good fortune. Although Nizam granted him the highest office available, Hassan was not prepared to settle for anything less than the chancellor's office. When this request was rejected, Hassan rebelled against the King and led a group of assassins who terrorized Persia for seventy years and eventually murdered Nizam ul Mulk. Later documents have proven, however, that this account has no historical authenticity.

2. *Rubaiyat,* translated by Edward Byles Colwell.

3. Edward FitzGerald, *The Rubáiyát of Omar Khayyám*

4. *Ibid.*

5. *Ibid.*

6. Nizami Aruzi, *Chahar Maqaleh,* published in Berlin, 1924, pp. 62–64.

7. Nizami Aruzi, *Chahar Maqaleh,* translated by E. G. Browne, Cambridge University Press, 1921, pp. 135–36.

8. *Qifti, History of the Philosophy,* edited by Julius Lipper, Leipzig, Germany, 1903, p. 243, translated by E. G. Browne.

9. Edward G. Browne, *Literary History of Persia,* vol. II, T. Fisher Unwin, London, 1906, pp. 254–55.

10. *Ibid.,* p. 258

11. E. H. Allen, *Edward FitzGerald's Rubaiyat of Omar Khayyam,* with original Persian sources, London, 1899, pp. xi–xii.

12. E. G. Browne, (translator), *Chahar Maqaleh,* Cambridge University Press, 1921, pp. 139–40.

13. E. H. Whinfield, *The Quatrain of Omar Khayyam,* London, 1883.

14. *Ibid.*

15. A. J. Arberry.

16. Translated by the authors.

17. Whinfield, *op. cit.*

18. Translated by A. J. Arberry.

19. Louisa Stuart Costello, *The Rose Garden of Persia,* T. N. Foulis, London, 1892, pp. 83–85.

20. *Ibid.,* pp. 83–84.

21. Translated by A. J. Arberry.

22. Whinfield, *op. cit.*

23. FitzGerald, *op. cit.*

24. Whinfield, *op. cit.*

25. Whinfield, *op. cit.*

26. Arberry, *op. cit.*

27. Whinfield, *op. cit.*

28. Kaikobad and Kaikhosru were the two famous Kings of Persia.

29. Hatim Tai was the legendary rich Arab Chief.

30. FitzGerald, *op. cit.*

31. FitzGerald, *op. cit.*

32. FitzGerald, *Rubaiyat, op. cit;* XI–XII

33. *Ibid.*

34. *Ibid.,* p. 16.

Index

241

Fikr (fortitude), 32
FitzGerald, E., 215, 222, 237
Franklin, Benjamin, 116
Frederick II, 87, 88

Gnosis, 36, 37, 38, 52, 54, 56
Gnostics, 42, 45, 53, 60
God: as Being, 34, 46, 81; existence, 67, 68; gratitude, 29; image, 60; love of, 36, 37, 140; union of, 38, 69
Goethe, 106, 118, 165, 169, 170, 171, 172, 173, 174, 175, 178, 179; *West-Eastern Divan,* 172, 173, 180
Greek philosophy, 63, 68, 76, 87, 224

Hassan al-Basri, 33, 63
Hafiz, 148–189; 61, 62, 115, 230; *Divan,* 151, 175, 180; theology, 148, 153
Hakim Sanai, 30
Homer, 153
Houris, 165
Hulul (doctrine of incarnation), 48, 60
human soul, 81, 82, 118
Hume, David, 90
Hussein Ibn Mansur Hallaj, 47, 48, 230

Iberian Peninsula, 20
Ibn-i-Roshd, 93
Ibn-i-Yamin, 51
Imadi Fagih, 154, 155
Iqbal, Muhammad, 105, 106
Iraq, 20
Isaiah, 58
Islam, 13, 21, 24, 28; God, 29; orthodoxy, 27; Sufi contribution, 47
Islamic law (Shariah), 45; community, 26, 27; doctrine, 59; philosophy, 148, 224

Jami, 54, 62, 118
Jerusalem, 33
Jesus, 20
Jews, 58, 86, 90, 92, 115

Jilani, Abdul Gader, 115
Jones, Sir William, 117
Judaism, 13, 40, 46

Kaaba, 44, 58
Kashmir, 181
Khayyam, Omar, 214–38; 61, 70; *Noruz Namah* (Persian New Year), 214, 215; Persian literature, 230; religion, 230, 231, 232, 233; *Rubaiyat,* 214, 222, 223, 237; *saki,* 218; on Sufism, 225
Khosrow, Nasir, 37
knowledge of God, 52

Le Galliene, R., 152
Lord Tennyson, Alfred, 215
Love: on religion, 30, 43, 52; on Sufism, 36, 63; virtue, 59
Lucretius, 237

Mahmud Shah, 156
Malik Shah, 76
Manichaenism, 46, 49, 60
Mansur Hallaj, 38
Marafat (gnosis) 37, 41
Mecca, 21, 44, 48, 167, 172
Medina, 172
Mongols, 127, 128
Moses, 87
Mubarizud Din, 153, 154, 155
Muhammad, Prophet, 27, 58, 79, 87, 92, 172; brotherhood, 58, 59; death of, 20; material renunciation, 34; teachings, 58, 60
Muhtasibi, 34
Muslims, 59, 78, 85, 87, 90
Muslim thought, 30, 33, 76, 83
Muzafferi Kings, 149
Mysticism, 14, 57, 62, 68, 69, 80, 83, 87, 231

Nehemiah, 58
Neo-Platonic ideas, 35, 60